Smart Discipline
for the Classroom

Dedicated to
Harold and Margaret Koenig—
Teachers of unconditional love

Smart Discipline
for the Classroom

*Respect and
Cooperation Restored*
Revised Edition

Larry Koenig

CORWIN PRESS, INC.
A Sage Publications Company
Thousand Oaks, California

For information address:

 Corwin Press, Inc.
A Sage Publications Company
2455 Teller Road
Thousand Oaks, California 91320
e-mail: info@corwin.sagepub.com

SAGE Publications Ltd.
6 Bonhill Street
London EC2A 4PU
United Kingdom

SAGE Publications India Pvt. Ltd.
M-32 Market
Greater Kailash I
New Delhi 110 048 India

Printed in the United States of America

Library of Congress Cataloging-in-Publication Data

Koenig, Larry.
    Smart discipline for the classroom : respect and cooperation
restored / Larry Koenig. — Rev. ed.
       p. cm.
    Includes bibliographical references.
    ISBN 0-8039-6341-6 (pbk.)
    1. School discipline—United States. 2. Classroom management—
United States.   I. Title.
LB3012.2.K64   1995
371.5'0973—dc20   95-22658

This book is printed on acid-free paper.

99 10 9 8 7 6 5 4 3   99-816

Interior illustrations by Phil Cangelosi
Cover design by Marcia R. Finlayson
First edition editor: Nydia Koenig
Corwin Press Production Editor: S. Marlene Head

Contents

Acknowledgments   vi

About the Author   vii

Introduction   1

1. Misbehaviors and Their Causes   7

2. Usual Discipline Methods and Their Drawbacks   12

3. Commonsense Principles of *Smart Discipline*   24

4. Effective Prevention Strategies   37

5. Strategies for Minor Misbehaviors ("Plan A")   60

6. Strategies for the Most Difficult Misbehaviors ("Plan B")   71

7. Attention Deficit Hyperactivity Disorder (ADHD) Strategies   90

8. Your Personal *Smart Discipline* Plan   105

Suggested Readings   112

Acknowledgments

I owe a debt of gratitude to many people who have contributed to this book in so many ways.

I want to thank Dr. Stephen Allen and Missy Allen for their thoughtful review of the book and their guidance in its revision. Also, my gratitude is extended to Cheryl White for the meticulous word processing and text design that was necessary in the creation of this book.

Especially, I would like to thank my wife, Nydia. Without her love, patience, inspiration, and hard work, *Smart Discipline for the Classroom* would not exist. My appreciation also goes to Ann McMartin, my editor at Corwin Press. Her skillful help in the editing process was invaluable. Victor Kirk has my appreciation for his diligent efforts in assisting with the review of the literature and help with compiling the excellent reading list at the end of the book.

About the Author

Larry Koenig is the executive director of the Up With Youth Company and a nationally known authority in the areas of discipline and parenting. Early in his career, he worked extensively with children and adolescents in a variety of settings, including classrooms, youth development centers, and psychiatric hospitals.

After 10 years as a practicing psychotherapist, Dr. Koenig founded the Up With Youth Company in 1985. It was one of the pioneering organizations in America devoted solely to the enhancement of self-esteem in young people. He has personally conducted workshops for more than 100,000 adolescents at the Up With Youth seminars. Additionally, he has trained more than 5,000 teachers in building self-esteem in young people and in classroom discipline.

Dr. Koenig is also the creator of the nationally acclaimed Up With Parents program. Hospitals, television stations, and schools nationwide have sponsored Up With Parents since 1986. This program focuses on the two topics about which parents most want information: self-esteem and discipline. Through these workshops he has established a reputation as one of the finest speakers in America today.

While working with students and classroom teachers throughout America, Dr. Koenig authored *Smart Discipline for the Classroom*. The demand for this program continues to grow as parents and teachers alike have become increasingly challenged by the task of teaching children in the 1990s.

Dr. Koenig is a recognized media personality, public speaker, and humorist. For 2 years, he has done a weekly parenting series for the ABC affiliate (WBRZ) in Baton Rouge, Louisiana. He is also frequently interviewed by television and radio stations throughout America. It is often said at his public appearances that Dr. Koenig has the unique ability to talk about exactly what is going on in today's classrooms and to give both meaningful and practical advice.

Dr. Koenig lives with his family in Baton Rouge, Louisiana. He may be contacted at 1-800-538-7107.

Introduction

The purpose of this book is to assist teachers in developing a personal plan of action to handle discipline in the classroom. Because of the plethora of misbehaviors in today's classroom, not having an effective discipline plan will thwart an instructor's goal of teaching. If you are a teacher, this needs no explanation. You already know how disruptive students can be.

Back in the dark ages of the 1950s and 1960s, all a teacher needed to be effective was a good lesson plan. In the 1990s, that's not enough. Now, a plan for handling behavior is also necessary. And it must be one that can:

1. Be individualized to fit each instructor's teaching style and personality

2. Prevent misbehaviors and encourage cooperation

3. Motivate a student to stop disruptive behaviors

4. Motivate a student to want to learn

5. Be quick and easy to use

Smart Discipline for the Classroom encompasses these goals. Also, you will find *Smart Discipline* adaptable to the different needs and personalities of children. More important, the system provides for "Plan A" and "Plan B" strategies that are progressive and always provide a "next step."

Plan A strategies are ones that take seconds to implement. They are quick and easy methods for both strengthening the teacher-student relationship and gaining immediate cooperation.

Plan B strategies take more time to implement but are designed to turn around the attitudes and behaviors of specific children. Most frequently, they will be used when Plan A methods have not produced satisfactory results.

All the strategies are presented in a logical progression. However, that does not mean they have to be used in that order—quite the contrary. *Smart Discipline* is designed with flexibility in mind. It is meant to let you pick and choose methods according to what fits for you in a given situation with a particular child.

Who Can Benefit From This Book?

Smart Discipline originally was written with teachers in mind. However, over the past several years a diversified audience has come to use the information. The list seems to be ever growing and now includes:

- School counselors
- Principals
- Teacher educators
- School secretaries
- School nurses
- Cafeteria workers
- Bus drivers
- Coaches
- Sunday school teachers
- Therapists
- Alcohol and drug counselors
- Foster parents
- Stepparents
- Police officers

This is a long list, but not a surprising one. All the people represented have a common need to relate to young people in a way that will motivate them to cooperate and accept guidance. In today's world, it is indeed a difficult task to gain the necessary cooperation from students of all ages—even young ones. The fact is that all of us who work with students are finding the task an increasing challenge.

We need all the help we can get to successfully meet this challenge and to guide children down a path toward success in life. The strategies and principles described in these pages are the stepping stones to meeting this important task with confidence.

Three Practical Considerations

I have presented the information contained in this book to groups of teachers all across America. Each time I do so, the feedback is overwhelmingly positive. However, several teachers in each location typically bring up one of three problems that they view as insurmountable. They describe the problems with statements such as:

> "Although I like the ideas, I don't have the time to use them. All of my time is taken up with trying to control the class, teaching, and paperwork."
>
> "My problem is that I have too many students for these ideas to be practical."
>
> "I've got a student in my class whose behavior is really rotten. I've tried everything and nothing works."

As these issues are recurring and very real, I would like to address each one at the outset.

Time is an issue for every teacher. And there always seem to be more and more things for teachers to do that take away from teaching time. *Smart Discipline* is not one of them, however. The effort invested in implementing these strategies will prevent discipline problems. This saves time in the long run.

Having an overload of students is also common. Some teachers have 100 or more students at a time to deal with in study hall or cafeteria settings. So, "How do I discipline a large group?" is a legitimate question.

The answer is, "You don't." Trying to discipline a group of any size is a losing battle. To be successful with discipline, it needs to be done on a one-to-one basis. And in reality, you will only need to use *Smart Discipline* with a few students. Get those cooperating with you and the rest will follow suit.

Last, there is the problem of what to do with the student who is resisting your best efforts (and driving you up the wall). One of the main reasons I have included a large variety of discipline strategies is because of this very problem.

To be successful with the most "difficult" discipline problems requires persistent, positive effort with a diverse assortment of techniques. With every student, something will work. For those of us who have chosen to work with students, it is our challenge to find out what that something is.

It is my hope that within these pages you will find what is needed to meet this challenge and put your students on the "superhighway toward success in school and in life."

What *Smart Discipline for the Classroom* Covers

Smart Discipline covers the following topics:

1. Disruptive behaviors and their causes
2. The usual approaches to discipline and their drawbacks
3. The commonsense principles on which *Smart Discipline* is based
4. Prevention strategies
5. Intervention strategies to motivate a student to stop disruptive behaviors and adopt productive behaviors
6. Attention deficit hyperactivity disorder (ADHD)—information and strategies that work
7. Designing a customized *Smart Discipline* plan to fit your needs

The *Smart Discipline* Advantages

- Retains teacher's authority
- Provides quick and easy solutions
- Adapts to different students
- Helps teacher stay calm and in charge

- Builds self-esteem
- Adapts to individual teaching styles
- Fosters behaviors conducive to learning
- Steers clear of power struggles
- Prevents misconduct
- Uses ADHD strategies
- Offers progressive steps
- Motivates students to pay attention
- Stops disruptive behaviors
- Builds strong teacher-student relationships
- Helps students successfully learn
- Helps teachers successfully educate
- Motivates respect for teachers, self, and others

As you can see, a lot is promised. The ultimate promise is that you will be able to take your plan into the classroom and achieve the results you need and want. If you cannot do this, I have failed in my purpose. But, in teaching and in learning, failure only comes to those who give up.

So, never—never—never give up!

Good luck!

1

Misbehaviors and Their Causes

Teaching is tough. Today's classrooms are populated with students exhibiting a wide variety of disruptive behaviors. Some examples follow. You may think of others.

_____	1. Shouting out	_____	21. Being disrespectful
_____	2. Passing notes	_____	22. Not completing work
_____	3. Cheating	_____	23. Stealing
_____	4. Making threats	_____	24. Hitting
_____	5. Committing violent acts	_____	25. Sleeping
_____	6. Swearing	_____	26. Teasing
_____	7. Talking back, sassing	_____	27. Playing pranks
_____	8. Wandering out of seat	_____	28. Insulting
_____	9. Throwing things	_____	29. Displaying negative attitude
_____	10. Skipping school	_____	30. Outbursts of anger
_____	11. Defying authority	_____	31. Indifference
_____	12. Hyperactivity	_____	32. Clowning
_____	13. Not following directions	_____	33. Arguing
_____	14. Crying	_____	34. Talking
_____	15. Interrupting	_____	35. Borrowing without asking
_____	16. Complaining constantly	_____	36. Showing bad manners
_____	17. Lying	_____	37. Being sarcastic
_____	18. Being late	_____	38. Being inattentive
_____	19. Throwing temper tantrums	_____	39. Dressing inappropriately
_____	20. Chewing gum	_____	40. Daydreaming
_____	Other: _____	_____	Other: _____
_____	Other: _____	_____	Other: _____

That's quite a list, isn't it? Almost overwhelming when you consider a teacher might have several students misbehaving in the same class. No wonder it's tough to teach sometimes. (Good thing we have many highly dedicated teachers in America.)

Because we'll need it later to customize a *Smart Discipline* Plan for you, please list the five behaviors that disrupt your class most frequently.

1. _____
2. _____
3. _____
4. _____
5. _____

Next, list the three most difficult behaviors for you to handle. They may be the same or different from those you listed above.

1. _____
2. _____
3. _____

Causes of Misbehaviors

When I conduct workshops around the country, a question frequently asked is "Why do you think there are so many more problems with behavior in school today compared to the way it was 20 or 30 years ago?" If I turn the question around and ask the workshop group what they think, there is a general consensus that two conditions are primarily to blame:

1. The breakup of the family
2. Lack of parental involvement and support in and for the schools

Undeniably, these two conditions have dramatically changed over the years, and, most certainly, behavior in the schools has been adversely affected.

A list of 5 or 10 behaviors is a manageable number.

But there are many other maladies that affect behavior and should also be taken into account.

_____ 1. Low self-esteem		_____ 16. Fetal alcohol syndrome
_____ 2. Drug abuse		_____ 17. Underachievement syndrome
_____ 3. ADD and ADHD		_____ 18. Poverty
_____ 4. Dysfunctional families		_____ 19. Attachment disorder
_____ 5. Childhood depression		_____ 20. Sociopathology
_____ 6. Child abuse		_____ 21. Prejudice
_____ 7. Sexual abuse		_____ 22. Anxiety
_____ 8. Oppositional disorders		_____ 23. Eating disorders
_____ 9. Alcoholism		_____ 24. Dyslexia
_____ 10. Gangs		_____ 25. Negative peer pressure
_____ 11. Family violence		_____ 26. Steroid abuse
_____ 12. Personality conflicts		_____ 27. Loss of hope
_____ 13. Puberty		_____ 28. Television sex and violence
_____ 14. Verbal abuse		_____ 29. Negative role models
_____ 15. Community violence		_____ Other: _____

This, too, is quite a list. All kinds of things can cause a child to act out in the classroom. It's important to know this so we don't take a child's misbehavior personally. If we take it personally, we will tend to respond emotionally rather than logically. Responding emotionally usually only makes the situation worse (more about this later). We need to be aware that on any given day, any student might act out in reaction to a personal problem and that we cannot fix all of their problems.

The good news is this: We can gain a student's cooperation anyway! In the next chapter, though, we'll look at the usual ways we use to correct behavior. We'll also explore their drawbacks.

As much as we would like to think our students
will "just say no," sometimes they don't. Consequently,
moods and behaviors in the classroom are adversely affected.

2

Usual Discipline Methods and Their Drawbacks

The discipline methods discussed in this section are the most prevalent ones used by our generation. They were not taught to us in school. For the most part, the discipline techniques we favor are the ones our parents and teachers used with us.

The funny thing is, we continue using them in the face of the evidence that:

1. Often, they did not work with us when we were growing up.

2. Often, they do not produce the expected results when we use them.

That we continue doing what does not work is an interesting phenomenon. Someone in Omaha once told me that the definition of insanity is expecting different results from the same behavior.

We continue ineffective behaviors for several reasons:

1. Behaviors learned through observation and mimicking become deeply ingrained.

2. Habits are tough to break (even in the face of profound logic that we should do so).

3. Ineffective methods sometimes work, and this leads us to believe they will work again if we are persistent.

The underlying problem is that sometimes the methods can both severely damage our relations with the child and even cause further acting out.

As we look at each of the most common discipline techniques, we will also look at why using them can work at cross-purposes with the goals of discipline. The goals of discipline are to motivate a student to:

1. Stop disruptive behaviors
2. Adopt productive behaviors
3. Desire to cooperate

Method: Lectures

Example: "Brad, I saw you throw your pencil at Kenny. I can't believe you would do such a stupid thing. Don't you realize you could hit him in the eye and blind him? How would you like it if someone poked your eye out with a pencil?"

Problems: Lecturing provides an emotional release for the lecturer but is usually ineffective in preventing further disruptive behaviors. Here's why. When a child is deciding whether or not to misbehave, three questions quickly pass through his or her mind:

1. Will I get caught?
2. Will I get punished?
3. Will I get out of it somehow?

All kids think they won't get caught. However, we really get into trouble when a student is answering the second question by thinking, "Even if I do get caught, I'm not going to get punished. Oh sure, I'll get yelled at and lectured to, but I won't really get punished." If a child is answering the question in this fashion, he or she will not likely be motivated to curtail future misbehaviors.

Also, when we lecture, the child may well feel "put down" or embarrassed. If that happens, watch out. This can cause a child to take his or her resulting anger and resentment out on you. The child's retaliation can lead to an ongoing battle that only escalates. If that happens, you know lecturing isn't working for you or the child.

Please note: Later chapters will reveal methods that work.

Method: Threats

Example: "Phyllis, you better straighten your act up, young lady, or you'll really be in trouble."

Problems: There are several drawbacks to threats. They include the following:

1. Threats are often made in anger, which usually fosters angry responses.
2. Power struggles that destroy cooperation may result.
3. Most threats are never carried out and kids know it.

Method: Rewards

Example: "Jerry, if you stay in your seat all morning, I will give/let you _____."

Problems: Rewards can motivate some children to behave on a short-term basis. However, no matter what reward you use to fill in the blank, you will sooner or later run into these difficulties:

1. The child may decide he or she no longer wants the reward, and so there is no incentive.
2. The child may come to expect rewards that you will neither be able nor willing to provide.
3. A reward system takes a lot of time to maintain.
4. Research clearly concludes that for rewards to be effective, they must be (a) immediate and (b) intermittent. Try to juggle this and teach at the same time!

In some settings, a reward system can be highly effective. The dilemma is that the variables needed are difficult to control in a classroom. Trying to do so often leaves both the teacher and the child frustrated.

Method: Punishment

Example: "I'm tired of you being late for class all the time. I've warned you enough and given you plenty of chances to be on time. Since you haven't, you will have to ____."

Problems: Providing consequences for misbehaving can be highly effective. However, to make them provide the results you want, certain guidelines must be followed. These will be discussed in the chapter on prevention strategies. In the meantime, let's look at the drawbacks if the guidelines are not followed.

1. Punishment causes some students to want revenge. Everyone loses then.

2. Students may say, "I don't care" or "So what?"

3. Students may manipulate us not to enforce the consequences. When this happens, we are in danger of setting a child up to think, "Even if I do get caught and get punished, I can crawfish my way out of it." Not good!

As human beings, we are known to be inconsistent with punishment. We will punish one time and not the next. We will even punish one child and not another. This can cause further problems in the classroom if students become vocal over inconsistencies and possible favoritism.

For discipline to work in the classroom, a well-thought-out system of rules and consequences must be in place. Impulsive and arbitrary punishment does not work. In fact, we can do more harm than good by punishing on the spur of the moment.

Method: Comparisons

Example: "Everyone, pay attention to how Jennifer is sitting quietly at her desk with her assignment done. Cindy, I want you especially to pay attention. If you would just act more like Jennifer, you would do a lot better in my class."

Problems: Some professionals in the areas of education and psychology advocate teachers' drawing attention to a child exhibiting the desired behavior and asking other students to follow suit. Sounds like a good idea, but:

1. The vast majority of kids hate to be publicly singled out for model behavior. It causes them to get labeled as nerds or teacher's pets. In short, they get rejected. When this happens, they try not to repeat the behaviors that got them singled out.

2. The natural response to being asked to be like someone else is "I'm not that person. I don't want to be that person. And I will not act like that person, no matter what."

When a younger sibling of a highly successful student comes to school, unfortunate and frequent comparisons occur. As comparisons continue to be made, the younger child commonly tries to establish his or her own identity by acting contrary to the older sibling. Or the child may even give up trying to succeed in school, thinking, "No matter how much effort I put in, I won't be able to achieve the success level of my brother, so why even try?" This, of course, is loser logic, but it happens. And it especially happens when "well-intended" comparisons are made.

Method: Anger

Anger doesn't sound like a discipline method, does it? But we use it like one.

Example: "You've got me really mad now. I can't wait to get hold of your parents. I'm going to give them an earful. I hope you get grounded for a month! Now, go back to your seat and stay there until I tell you to leave."

Problems: Angry outbursts work for us sometimes. At least, they can frequently get immediate results. The sheer force of energy in the emotion can frighten a child into compliance. However, we must watch out for the aftereffects:

1. Anger begets anger. You can expect an angry response at some point. How it comes back to you will be destructive. You can count on it. Unfortunately, you won't know when or where it will manifest itself.

2. There is a direct relationship between anger and reason. The more anger in an exchange, the less reason.

3. Some kids love to "push a teacher's buttons" to get the teacher angry. They think it's funny. Worse, they perceive the teacher to be out of control and themselves in control.

4. When we respond with anger, we sometimes say and do things we later regret (but can't take back). Being human, you know what I mean. It happens to all of us.

Method: Criticism/Reverse Psychology

Example: "You know what your problem is, Greg? Your problem is that you're just plain lazy. I told you to have your homework done by this morning. But you didn't do it, did you? No, you didn't. The problem with you is that you're just plain lazy and you are never going to amount to anything."

Problems: We learned this technique from our parents' generation. It is based on a theory that reasons: "If you point out evidence to another person that he or she has a character defect, the person will change." In our generation, we call this logic "reverse psychology." It's a slight variation of the belief that "if you tell people they can't do something, that will cause them to do it."

All of us can cite numerous examples of how our use of criticism caused someone to change his or her behavior. Sure it can work, but using criticism is playing with dynamite for the following reasons:

1. Criticism destroys relationships. Human beings, young and old, hate to be criticized. It makes us angry and resentful, and it makes us criticize right back.

2. Criticism can cause another person to refuse to cooperate with us. It even riles feelings of hate, especially in students with low self-esteem.

3. Criticism cultivates and reinforces negative beliefs. When we point out someone's negative behavior and ascribe it to a character fault, we may well cause that person to believe that is "just the way I am." The person then continues to act that way.

When we use criticism, we do so because of a good intention to help a person change or because we are angry at the person. Either way, criticism can erode relationships and self-esteem.

Method: Corporal Punishment

Example: Student misbehaves and the teacher sends the student to the principal's office. The principal spanks the child.

Problems: In some ways, I hate to even broach the issue of corporal punishment. It's a no-win situation because people have strong opinions on both sides of the issue. Their minds are already made up.

I'm against it for the following reasons:

1. If you spank a child, you run the risk of making an enemy for life, an enemy who will seek revenge.

2. Some kids couldn't care less if they get spanked. In fact, they prefer it. It lets them off the hook by leading them to think, "I can do anything I want because even if I get caught, the worst that will happen is a spanking."

3. Corporal punishment is now illegal in many states.

You can take your chances with criticism, but you'll always lose.

No matter how we personally view it, the whole issue of corporal punishment is a dead issue. Society in general no longer condones it, and school boards will not allow it. These stances are not likely to change in the foreseeable future.

Method: The Vulcan Pinch

Example: Student acts out and the teacher maneuvers around behind the student to execute a pinch of the trapezoid muscle.

Problems: I just know a number of you are thinking, "Who would do such a thing in this day and age?" Others are thinking, "What's the big deal? It's quick and easy and it works." If you're an advocate of the Vulcan Pinch, consider the following:

1. The infliction of physical pain causes anger, feelings of hate, and a desire for revenge. In no way will it instill in a child a positive desire to cooperate with you.
2. A well-intentioned motivational pinch can cause the loss of a job and create a lawsuit to boot.

The answer to the question, "Who would do such a thing in this day and age?" is "Lots of us." But we need to stop it.

Method: Commands

Example: "Go back to your seat right now! And take off those sunglasses immediately!"

Problems: The older the student, the less likely this will work. You might get away with barking an order at a primary student, but when a child attains the age of ten, watch out! As a result of making commands, you are likely to generate problems such as:

1. A student may respond with, "Make me." However you respond at this point, whether you enter into a power struggle

or back down, you will lose and so will the student. (Why power struggles must be avoided at all costs will be dealt with extensively later.)

2. The student may respond with "Why?" Two likely responses to this are either "Because I said so" or "The reason why." Students resent the first response and argue with the second. Some kids, by the way, love nothing better than to lure a teacher into a good argument. Once it starts, everyone loses.

3. The student may respond to your command by ignoring you and acting as if you didn't even say anything. We then repeat the command more loudly, which begets a blank stare from the student (which says, "Who, me?"). This aggravates us to the point we may say something like "Yes, you, you big dummy!" From here, there is no good way to go.

One thing common to adults and kids alike is their dislike for being ordered to do something. We all resist this approach to some degree. Try it with a strong-willed and oppositional child and it will end in disaster. More about how to avoid this later.

Method: Notes to Parents

Example:

Dear Mrs. Greene,

Your daughter Mandy is being disruptive in class and her homework assignments are consistently incomplete. Please do whatever you can to rectify this situation. Please let me know if you have questions.

Sincerely,

Mrs. Bunker

Problems: Notes can be highly effective but there are several pitfalls. They include the following:

1. The note may never get home.

2. If Mrs. Greene is an all-American mother, she will ask Mandy what's going on. If Mandy is an all-American girl, she will explain to her mother that it is not her fault. She will blame the other kids and say, "But the real problem is the teacher—she doesn't like me and is always picking on me."

3. Chances are that the parents will give Mandy a good lecture and that will be the end of it.

If your notes aren't getting results, it is probably because of one of these pitfalls.

Method: Principal's Office

Example: Student acts out in class and is asked to go to the principal's office. Teacher sends along a note that says:

> Charles has been disruptive in class all period. He has been uncooperative and disrespectful. This includes being out of his seat, talking, and using vulgarity. Thank you.
>
> Mrs. Simms

Problems: One common drawback in sending a student to the principal's office is that the whole class gets the message that you are not the ultimate authority, the principal is. As we'll see later, it's possible to get the principal involved in the solution process without giving up authority. In the meantime, before you send a student to the principal, as in my example, consider these issues:

1. Children lie. It's a fact, and they will paint their own picture of reality especially when confronted by a principal.

2. It is difficult for a principal to effectively handle a situation without knowing what actually happened.

3. The principal's resolution will be questioned when the student returns to class. The offender will be asked by friends, "What happened?" to which the child will respond, "Principal didn't do nothing to me; it was no big deal!" Inevitably, you will lose face with the class.

There are several powerful ways to solve behavioral problems by involving the principal while the teacher remains the authority figure for the students. These will be dealt with in detail in chapter 5.

Before we get to these strategies and others, in the next chapter we'll discuss the principles on which the strategies are founded, plus some highly effective prevention principles.

3

Commonsense Principles
of *Smart Discipline*

This chapter will deal with the principles behind the prevention and intervention strategies that follow. I call them commonsense principles because they make sense to me. They evolved out of my work with thousands of kids all over America in a variety of settings: classrooms, family counseling, reform schools, psychiatric hospitals, and my Up With Youth Program.

Although these principles make a lot of sense to me, you will have to make up your own mind. None of them, you will find, is new. All have been passed down to us through the ages in one fashion or another.

Principle 1: Change Happens Both Quickly and Slowly

Some students will respond immediately to discipline methods. Some respond so quickly and completely that what you are doing may seem like magic. Others respond so slowly that we conclude our methods aren't working.

As a general rule, we should commit to a plan of action for at least a month before we give up and try something else. Remember that more is accomplished in life through sheer persistence than anything else.

Principle 2: Methods That Work for Some Students Won't Work for Others

Kids, as you know, are different. It is surprising when an approach that works wonders with one child doesn't work with another. The common human response to this is irritation. It aggravates us when children are unresponsive to our positive efforts. I think it might be because a nonresponse or negative response makes us feel rejected or unappreciated.

Whatever the feelings when your efforts fail, they are natural and to be expected. The most common reaction is to respond negatively to the child. This is also the most common mistake. A more positive strategy is to be ready with another positive approach.

Principle 3: A Well-Thought-Out Personal Discipline Plan Is Essential

In today's schools, some things are for certain. One is that some students will misbehave. Unfortunately, the number of students who misbehave is growing, as is the variety and severity of misbehaviors.

Not having a well-thought-out plan of how to handle these misbehaviors is as foolhardy as teaching without a lesson plan. Or, if you prefer, it would be like going out to coach a game without a game plan. The results of either are less than satisfactory.

Confronting misbehavior without a discipline plan will also yield less-than-satisfactory results. Without a plan, we naturally resort to the discipline methods with which we were raised. Many of these, as described in chapter 2, not only don't work but actually foster more misbehavior.

Having a well-thought-out discipline plan will produce both the desired results and a feeling of confidence. Suffice it to say, having a sound discipline plan will help you attain your ultimate goal: that is, *to teach!*

Principle 4: Adults Give Positive Students Positive Feedback and Negative Students Negative Feedback

Although there are exceptions, for the most part we are conditioned to respond to positive children with delightful and encouraging comments. When this happens between teacher and student, several things occur:

1. The child's desire to cooperate with the teacher increases.
2. The child's desire to learn from the teacher increases.

3. The teacher helps the child believe that the child "has what it takes" to be successful in school.

Unfortunately, we are conditioned to respond to negative children with sometimes demeaning and discouraging remarks. We do so because their behavior is irritating to us and because we believe that by pointing out the "errors of their ways" we will motivate them to change. When teachers take this approach, the following is likely to occur:

1. The child's desire to cooperate with the teacher decreases.
2. The child's desire to learn from the teacher decreases.
3. The teacher helps the child believe that the child "doesn't have what it takes" to be successful in school.

Someday soon (maybe today will be the day), we will realize that negative responses to children only perpetuate negative behavior. To be honest, many of us have realized this. However, we continue responding negatively because we have been conditioned to react in this way and have not yet found a new approach that works for us.

Principle 5: Using the Same Discipline Methods Over and Over Will Yield the Same Results. Therefore, If You Wish to Change the Results, You Must Change Discipline Methods

This, I know, sounds rather elementary. However, as humans we often get stuck in a rut. What happens is that we try something with a student one time and it works. The next ten times it doesn't, but we keep it up because we reason that if it worked once, it should work again.

When we are unsuccessful in getting a child to modify or change a behavior, we do something rather silly. We blame the child. Or we blame the parents, or the socioeconomic conditions, or TV, or the phase of the moon for that matter.

Although we need to give strategies a fair chance to work, sometimes, in order to engineer positive results, we need to change discipline strategies.

Principle 6: The More a Student Acts Out, the More the Student Will Benefit From a Well-Thought-Out Positive Plan of Action

Typically, children who act out at school are getting negative feedback and criticism heaped on them both at school and at home. When this happens, students usually respond with anger or depression, neither of which is conducive to learning.

What a shock it is to a negative student to have someone respond consistently with a positive approach. In fact, one teacher doing so can sometimes totally turn a student around.

Principle 7: Students Will Often Act Worse in Response to Positive Approaches

There is a reason for this: Children are like a lot of grown-ups. That is, they like things to remain the same because they know what to expect and how to respond. Changes, therefore, frequently cause harsh and negative reactions meant to result in a return to old and familiar patterns.

Also, kids like to conduct their own research. They like to test things out to see if the change in response is "for real" or not. We must expect negative reactions and pass "the test" by responding with positive interventions even in the face of negative feedback from the student.

Although we need to change the discipline techniques that aren't working with a particular student, we must resist the natural urge to respond negatively to a student who responds negatively to our positive efforts. Rather, when we have determined after a couple of weeks that a particular strategy is not working we need to be ready with another constructive approach.

In the meantime, anticipate negative reactions and keep your responses positive!

Principle 8: Behaviors That We Pay Attention to Are Reinforced

This explains a mystery. It gives us the reason why we often fail miserably when we try so hard to change a child's behavior.

What I mean is this: All children thrive on attention. And all children try to garner attention through positive behavior and achievements. Some are successful and some are not. Those who aren't successful through positive means learn very quickly to get attention by acting out. The attention they get, of course, simply motivates them to continue acting out.

Even though we understand this and have talked about it among ourselves many times, we get sucked right into participating in this negative cycle anyway. The only way out of it is to follow the Boy Scout motto and "be prepared" with a positive plan of action. (Please note: Have patience, we are going to start putting together just such a plan in the next chapter.)

Principle 9: People Treat Us the Way We Treat Them

We are all familiar with this principle. It is also one we teach to children. We tell them, "If you want people to be nice to you, then you must be nice to them."

This is even a principle that we put into practice for the most part. Unfortunately, we tend to throw it out the window when someone is being nasty to us. Nastiness causes us to be mean right back. Once we do so, a negative cycle gets set into motion that is tough to break. Maybe this is why someone very wise once advised: Turn the other cheek.

When we turn the other cheek, we need to be ready with a positive response, one that bespeaks of kindness, concern, and compassion. The payoff will come in setting in motion a positive cycle that also will be hard to break.

Principle 10: Some Kids Irritate Us

The opposite is also true. Some kids delight us. Of course, we get along well with these kids. We just seem to hit it off with them. Discipline with these kids is rarely a problem. For one thing, they want to behave for us. We also overlook minor indiscretions because we like them.

Woe unto the child, though, who irritates us. With this child we typically are hypercritical and unforgiving. Some would say it is because these children are displaying the flaws that we dislike (or hate) in ourselves.

Our upbeat moods uplift those around us.

Whatever the reason, it is beneficial to face up to our humanness and realize that some kids will always rub us the wrong way. Benefits are achieved by allowing ourselves to be human while purposely deciding to resolve these personality conflicts with a positive plan of action.

Principle 11: Anger Blocks Learning

Think about this for a moment: Would you buy something from someone with whom you are angry? Not on your life. In fact, we will do whatever it takes to avoid doing business with that person. Kids are the same way with their teachers. No way will a student "buy" what the teacher is selling if he or she is angry with the teacher.

What the child will do instead is fill his or her mind with:

1. Thoughts of revenge
2. Thoughts of how unfair the teacher is
3. Plans of how the child can convince everyone else how wicked the teacher is

When the student's mind is busy with these thoughts, the learning process becomes solidly blocked.

Later chapters will reveal ways to both prevent and overcome anger.

Principle 12: Teaching Is Not a Popularity Contest

I mention this because I can predict that at this point, some teachers are thinking, "I'm not teaching to make friends with my students" and "Why should I have to walk around on eggshells so I don't hurt anyone's feelings?"

The reason is that if it is your goal to teach, then you must pay attention to your students and develop a positive relationship between yourself and them. Students will not learn from or cooperate with a teacher whom they perceive as unfriendly, uncaring, and disrespectful.

No, teaching is not a popularity contest, but it is a fact that the stronger the teacher-student relationship, the more the student will (a) behave, (b) learn from the teacher, and (c) accept correction. Knowing this, we can put it to work for us so we will be more effective teachers.

Principle 13: Issues Should Be Dealt With on a Feeling Level Outside the Classroom

For the past couple of decades, we have been taught to resolve difficulties with other people by "expressing our feelings." My generation (the baby boomers) has not learned how to do this very well. We need to keep practicing until we get it right. Repressed feelings have a way of coming back to haunt us.

But, as with everything, there is a time and a place. The place not to express negative feelings is in the classroom—at least not at the time we are feeling them. When we are in the midst of a raw emotion, we tend to say and do things we regret later. And we tend to spark emotional responses in the person with whom we are communicating. When this happens, nobody wins. Everyone loses.

A far more productive strategy is to "stay in your head" and deal with conflicts on an intellectual level in the classroom. The expression of feelings should be confined to a one-on-one basis away from other students—after everyone has calmed down. How feelings can be used effectively with students will be dealt with under the segment titled "Deliver 'I' Messages" later in this book (p. 86).

Principle 14: Children Are Purveyors of Misinformation

This is a polite way of stating the fact that many children lie on occasion, which is not to say that all children are liars.

The point is this: We can expect children to lie to protect themselves. Therefore, we can expect them to lie when we ask them questions about their involvement in misdeeds. It is only natural for them to do so as an act of self-preservation. (Please note: Yes, I know there are some kids who are exceptionally honest.)

Although realizing children are prone to lying, we adults do an absurd thing. We question them, send them to the principal or home with a note, expecting them to tell the truth. Of course, they often do not tell the truth. We then do something even more absurd: We get angry at them for lying.

We need to find ways to confront negative behavior while encouraging honesty.

Principle 15: Power Struggles Must Be Avoided at All Costs

Power struggles between teachers and students always end badly. The older the student, the worse the outcome. In the 1990s, these power struggles are apt to end in the student committing defiant acts, such as

1. Swearing
2. Hitting
3. Stabbing
4. Shooting

That's the bad news. The good news is that there are numerous ways to gain a student's cooperation without getting into a power struggle. All of the discipline strategies in chapters 4, 5, 6, and 7 focus on accomplishing just that.

Principle 16: Words Are Powerful

Words are powerful because they are the seeds from which beliefs grow. Let me explain by describing the step-by-step process of how beliefs are formed.

When children are growing up, they are trying to answer a subconscious question that goes something like this: "Who am I; what makes me different from everyone around me?" As children seek answers, they listen to information about themselves from other people. As children obtain information, they draw conclusions about themselves and look around for evidence to support the conclusions (which they normally find). Children then integrate the conclusions into their self-talk and belief system. Once this happens, children act according to their beliefs.

Here's an example. A teacher hands a math paper back to a student and says, "Look, Brad, you got an A. I think you have a natural ability for math." Brad, of course, feels pretty good about this so he studies his math even harder and ends up with an A on his report card. Quite naturally he thinks, "My teacher is right; I am good in math." He then continues to affirm his belief by taking additional math courses in order to improve his math skills.

Self-esteem is molded mainly by feedback from adults.

It's as simple as that. A teacher can point out something to a student once and give life to a belief that will last a lifetime. Words are that powerful!

Principle 17: Students Act According to Their Beliefs

Once individuals adopt beliefs, the beliefs guide both their behaviors and their decisions. Trying to get a person to act contrary to a belief is difficult at best.

This explains why traditional approaches to modifying behavior often fail. If, for instance, a child picks up a belief like "I don't have what it takes to be successful in school," then it does not matter how wonderful a system of rules, rewards, and consequences you have. You will not be successful in implementing the learning process in that child.

A child who believes that he or she can't be successful in school usually seeks out the company of other students who have decided the same thing. They support one another in the belief that "school is for nerds and doesn't matter anyway." This belief frees them to devote 100% of their time to being disruptive in the classroom.

What a mess this causes for the teacher! These students now have absolutely nothing to lose. Threats of punishment and banishment become a big joke to them.

To reach these kids, radical steps must be taken to instill beliefs that "they have what it takes to be successful in school" and "success in school will enable them to get what they want out of life." Helping a student adopt these two beliefs is probably one of the best things we can ever do for the student. Without these, the child is lost and so are all of our efforts to guide that child's behavior in the classroom.

Principle 18: Success Is Dependent on Encouragement

Every single human being needs encouragement. Without it, we give up. Unfortunately, students with significant behavior problems overwhelmingly receive negative and discouraging feedback. After a time, they give up.

When I talk about this, many teachers say, "But what are we to do when so much of this negativity is being heaped on the child at home?" The answer is "a lot." A teacher should never underestimate his or her potential to positively affect a student's life.

Talent's not inherited—it's encouraged.

I am reminded every single day of people who attribute their success in life to teachers who took the time and effort to encourage them. The less support the child is receiving at home, the greater the impact of a teacher's encouragement.

Principle 19: "An Ounce of Prevention Is Worth a Pound of Cure"

Ben Franklin

In reference to classroom discipline, this famous quote holds true. Once a child enters into a pattern of misbehavior, it takes a concentrated effort to turn it around.

The good news is disruptive behavior can be prevented. It can be thwarted with friendliness, concern, and respect. When students perceive civil treatment from a teacher, they will bend over backwards to cooperate. And they will even provide peer pressure for others in the class to follow suit.

The more effort put into developing teacher-student relationships, the less effort will be needed to correct misbehavior. Because prevention is critical, the whole next chapter will be devoted to the specifics of how this can be accomplished.

Principle 20: Teachers Have a Powerful Effect on People's Lives

Behind every single successful human being there exists a group of dedicated teachers. They not only taught the student but provided discipline, motivation, and encouragement. Teachers provide the foundation on which success is built.

I mention this not just as a positive stroke but as a fact for teachers to keep in mind when the going gets tough with a particular student. The more negative and defiant the student, the more he or she stands to benefit from a persistently positive approach from the teacher. A positive stance can literally save a child from oblivion.

The rule to keep in mind is this: The more irritated, aggravated, or hopeless a student makes you feel, the more that child needs your positive influence in his or her life. And never, never forget how important being a teacher is. The very foundation of our modern world depends on teachers, as does the future success of each and every individual student.

4

Effective Prevention Strategies

Prevention strategies are meant to instill a personal desire in students to behave in the classroom. They are also meant to create a positive atmosphere in the classroom that will be conducive to both teaching and learning.

Although little time needs to be spent employing prevention strategies, it is beneficial to detail a plan of methods you will use and commit yourself to using them. For positive, upbeat, and enthusiastic teachers, this will be easy. For the rest, it's a little tougher.

It's tougher if the teacher is:

1. Used to handling things as they come up
2. Personally uncomfortable with displaying extroverted behaviors
3. Convinced that time is not available to carry out the prevention strategies
4. Comfortable with the way things are and sees no reason to change

These all are powerful reasons. I know change is tough and only those with a strong personal desire will change.

Please keep in mind as you go through the prevention strategies that some will appeal to you and others will not, and some you may already use. Those that appeal to you should be noted in your personal *Smart Discipline* Plan at the end of this book.

Each of the prevention methods is simple. However, each has the potential of encouraging students to

1. Cooperate with you and other teachers
2. Desire to learn and be guided by you

Strategy: Welcome Students

Examples:

A. Welcome students at the door with either a verbal greeting or a handshake.
B. Tell a few students each day, "I'm glad you're here."
C. Greet a few students each day by putting a hand on their shoulders and saying something like, "Jim, how are you today?"

Notes: This simple idea produces radical results. Admittedly, it takes some time but the payoff for the effort is large. Students will get the idea from your welcoming them that you care about them personally. This knowledge fosters a desire to cooperate.

One note of caution about touching. Some students may pull away. However, the risk can be well worthwhile. A pat on the shoulder can establish a link between a teacher and student that will have a powerful and positive impact on the student.

Strategy: Express Appreciation

Instructions: First, check off from the list below the behaviors and qualities that are the most important to you for students to display.

_____ Follows directions		_____ Enthusiastic
_____ Positive attitude		_____ Respectful
_____ Honesty		_____ Prompt
_____ Self-confidence		_____ Completes work
_____ Good manners		_____ Organized
_____ Good listener		_____ Attentive
_____ Friendly		_____ Sharing
_____ Trustworthy		_____ Volunteers
_____ Displays initiative		_____ Polite
_____ Sincere		_____ Cheerful
_____ Considerate		_____ Loyal
_____ Sense of humor		_____ Persistent
_____ Ambitious		_____ Goal-oriented
_____ Creative		_____ Kind
_____ Self-reliant		_____ Understanding
_____ Dependable		_____ Hard worker
_____ Calm		_____ Cooperative
_____ Determined		_____ Good memory
_____ Other: _____		_____ Other: _____

Next, on a note card list the behaviors and characteristics that you assign the highest priority (up to ten). Place this card where you will automatically see it on a daily basis.

Then, say to a few students each day things such as:

- "Good job on staying in your seat today. . . . I appreciate it."
- "Thank you for being honest with me today."
- "I appreciated it when you came back to class right on time."
- "I'm proud of you for being persistent with getting your assignment done."
- "Thank you for being so cooperative today. . . . You made my day go better."
- "I noticed how hard you worked on getting along with your classmates today; thank you."

Notes: When you make these comments, be sure to say them to the student either in private or in a low voice. Except for a few students with exceptional self-esteem, most tend to get embarrassed when singled out for exemplary behavior. In fear of being labeled a nerd or teacher's pet, many students will even extinguish positive behaviors likely to single them out for public attention.

However, all students thrive on appreciation and positive feedback given in private. Such experiences not only foster future cooperation but self-esteem as well. Positive feedback especially helps a student foster a belief that he or she has what it takes to succeed in school.

For optimum effect, keep your feedback short and sweet, and couple it with some evidence of the behavior or characteristic on which you are focusing. And don't pay any attention if the student rejects your positive comments. Secretly, these students greatly appreciate these comments, and their negative response is a cover-up for embarrassment.

If you encounter a negative response, do not try to force your point. Simply say, "I just wanted you to know," and walk away with a smile.

Strategy: Write a Note

Instructions: Use the same examples from the last segment on appreciation, and convey them in a note to the student. Be sure to

1. Keep it simple
2. Keep it short
3. Base it on behavior you have observed
4. Say "thank you" in some fashion

Strategy: Write a Letter

Instructions: Same as above, but address it to the student's parents. Set a goal to send one letter home per week. Ask the school to spring for the postage.

Would you have liked more praise when you were a child?
Could your students use some more too?

Example:

Dear Mr. and Mrs. Thompson:

I thought you would like to know how cooperative James has been in my class. Today I especially appreciated how well he followed directions and completed his work.

Let me know if I can ever answer any questions for you about James's school work.

Sincerely,

Ms. Cindy Preston

Notes: The biggest objection to this is the time that it takes. But it takes less time than you might think. If you use basically the same letter and keep it short, this should take less than 5 minutes per week.

You can do yourself a major favor by making sure that you send these letters home first to the parents of the students you are having the most difficulty with. It will not only help encourage positive behavior but will likely enlist the parents as allies as well. This way, if you do have to call home later to discuss a problem, you will most likely get a much more positive response.

To save time, do your letters on a computer so you don't have to rewrite them each time.

For future reference, you may want to keep copies.

What an impact these letters will make! I can just see all the smiles, feel all the warm feelings, and predict all the resulting good behavior already.

Strategy: Call Home

Instructions: Instead of writing a positive note to the parents, call them. Stick to the same rules as described with sending a note, but add one thing: Smile when you are talking on the phone. They won't be able to see it, but they will be able to sense your enthusiasm.

Remember to keep the conversation focused on the positives. If negatives come up, explain that the purpose of your call was to express your appreciation and that you would be happy to call another time to help solve any difficulties. For the most part, you won't have to worry about this happening as most parents will be so thrilled with your positive call that they won't bring up problems. Be sure to keep a phone log to record information learned in these calls.

Strategy: Ask Personal Questions

Instructions: Start asking different students questions that will help you get to know them personally. For example,

1. "Do you have a pet?" If so, ask what kind; if not, ask, "What kind would you like to have if you could have one?"

2. "How do you get to school?" and "How long does it take?"

3. "What's your favorite color?"

4. "Who is your best friend?"

5. "What's your favorite sport or hobby?"

Don't expect to keep the answers in memory. Write them down in a notebook later so you can refer to them and follow up with comments such as:

1. "How's your dog Pete doing?"

2. "Did you get wet walking to school today or were you able to get a ride?"

3. "I see you're wearing your favorite color today."

4. "What have you and your friend Sue been up to lately?"

5. "Have you been in any good volleyball games lately?"

Notes: Taking a personal interest in students' lives motivates students to take an interest in learning from and cooperating with the teacher. Also, a student who has experienced a teacher's personal interest is more likely to accept correction from that teacher.

Strategy: Transpose Critical Comments

Instructions: Review the sample destructive criticisms and their alternatives below. Then fill out the blanks under "Your turn."

Destructive Criticisms and Sample Alternatives

Criticism	Sample Alternative
You're lazy.	You're a hard worker and I expect you to act that way.
You're a liar.	You are an honest child and I expect you to tell me the truth.
All you ever do is complain.	I handle complaints by appointment only. Would you like to make an appointment?
You're just plain mean. If I catch you hitting again, you'll be sorry.	Hitting is not allowed. I have made an appointment for you to talk to me about it at 3:15.
You've got the worst manners of anyone I know.	Earlier today I saw you using good manners. Would you consider using your good manners right now? Thank you.
Your attitude stinks. In fact, with an attitude like that, you will never amount to anything.	You seem like you're in a bad mood right now. It's not always easy to be positive, but a good attitude goes a long way with me.

Your turn: _____   _____

_____   _____

_____   _____

Notes: It's tough to stop using criticism. Using criticism to shape behavior is habitual in our culture. Changing to a positive approach takes some forethought, planning, and practice. Every bit of effort you put into it is well worthwhile as criticism is guaranteed to destroy a teacher-student relationship and spawn a desire for revenge.

As you seek a more positive approach, keep in mind that you will most likely slip up from time to time and criticize. Don't beat yourself up over it, but rather decide how you will handle the situation next time.

Remember, though, never to criticize a student in front of other students. To do so is to drop an H-bomb on any hopes you have of gaining this child's cooperation.

Strategy: Point Out Talents

Instructions: Pay attention to the strengths that individual students have and point them out to a few students each day.

Examples:

- "Trisha, you have a good sense of organization. I like the way you organized your thoughts in the report on the Civil War."
- "Bill, one of your talents seems to be in math. Last week you got a B- on your final exam. You're getting better all the time."
- "Lynn, I heard from Ms. Brooks that you are one of her best music students. She thinks you have a natural talent for music."
- "Good speech, John. It was concise and to the point. Seems like you're a natural when it comes to speaking."

Notes: When you point out the evidence that a student has a specific talent, wonderful things happen. The student becomes motivated to work harder to develop that talent and builds a belief that says, "I have what it takes to be successful in school." And, of course, anyone who helps that student feel this way will gain the student's cooperation.

Choose your words carefully.
Children take them for being true and construct beliefs out of them.

Please remember that giving positive reinforcement should, if possible, be done in private. Private comments are taken to heart and have a powerful impact without getting the child labeled as teacher's pet.

Strategy: Predict Success

Instructions: These are the same as in "Point Out Talents," plus adding a prediction of success.

Examples:

- "Trisha, with your talent for organization, you'll go far. I wouldn't be surprised if you become a successful business manager one day."
- "Bill, you continue to improve in math. You know, you could be a math teacher!"
- "Lynn, with your talent for music, I bet you could have a successful career using your musical talents one day."
- "John, someday you're going to speak in front of large groups and get paid lots of money for it."

Notes: Don't worry if the student shrugs off your comments. You can count on a good share of the students taking your predictions to heart and living up to them.

Strategy: Make Appointments

Instructions: Whenever a student has a complaint or wants to argue a point, make an appointment to discuss the matter at a time you can speak in private. At the appointment, ask the student to explain his or her point of view. Clarify the child's perception, empathize with it, and state your decision. Keep the appointment under 5 minutes in length.

By predicting a student's success, you help create
a self-fulfilling prophecy. As a bonus, encouragement fosters cooperation.

Example:

Student: "Ms. Brooks, you treated me unfairly. Why did you take 5 points off for listing my textbook as a reference?"

Teacher: "John, that sounds like a complaint. I would like to give your complaint serious consideration, so let's make an appointment to talk about it. I have an opening at 12:45 or 3:00. Which would be better for you?"

Student: "I don't want any appointment. I want to know now!"

Teacher (smiling): "I understand you would like to discuss it now, but I handle all legitimate complaints by appointment. Would 12:45 be OK or would 3:00 be better?"

Student: "12:45, I suppose, will be OK."

Teacher: "I'm glad you came in, John. I appreciate your willingness to put off talking about your complaint until we could sit down together. Tell me what the problem is."

Student: "The problem is that you took off 5 points for using my textbook as one of my three references for my report. That's not fair 'cause you never said we couldn't do that."

Teacher: "Let me see if I understand you. You're upset because I docked you for using your text as a reference, and you think this is unfair because you didn't hear me say this wasn't allowed. Is that right?"

Student: "Yeah, that's it and I want my 5 points back."

Teacher: "I can see that those 5 points are very important to you. And you are right that it would be unfair for me to take off the points without warning. Unfortunately, John, I did tell the class about this. I'm sorry you didn't hear me. Because I did mention it, John, I won't be able to give your points back."

Student: "But that's not fair!"

Teacher: "Yes, I understand you don't feel I'm being fair. However, I want you to know I really mean it when I say I appreciate your willingness to sit down and talk with me about it. Thank you." (Teacher, if comfortable with it, shakes hands with the student or pats the student on the back.)

Notes: There are some major advantages to using the "Appointment Strategy." They include the following:

1. Prevents power struggles

2. Provides cool-down period

3. Avoids embarrassment for teacher and student

4. Gives teacher time to think out responses

5. Gives students message that their issues will be taken seriously

6. Reduces the number of frivolous complaints as only students serious about their point will tend to go to the trouble of coming in for an appointment

Strategy: Elicit Third-Party Encouragement

Instructions: Ask other teachers to observe your students around school and to report any good behavior to you. As you receive the reports, pass along what you heard to the individual students in private.

Examples:

- "Jerry, Ms. Kramer mentioned to me how you talked Jimmy out of fighting on the playground. Good job!"

- "Mr. Powers pulled me aside this morning in the staff meeting and told me about how you helped him clean up the mess in the hallway yesterday after school. Keep up the good work!"
- "Shelly, Ms. Perkins sure had some good things to say about you today. I'm proud of you for being such a positive student."

Notes: Please keep in mind that in our society, 99% of the positive feedback goes to well-behaved kids with positive attitudes. Certainly, they should continue to get their share of attention, but it is the "problem children" we need to turn around. Therefore, it behooves us to make a concerted effort to bring loads of positive feedback their way. Every bit we can funnel their way increases their chance for success in school and their desire to behave appropriately.

Strategy: List Misplaced Behaviors

Instructions: Tell the class that a misplaced behavior is a behavior that is perfectly appropriate somewhere else but not in the class. Brainstorm with the class what some of these behaviors are and list them on the blackboard.

Your list should end up looking something like this:

1. Running
2. Yelling
3. Interrupting
4. Talking out of turn
5. Engaging in horseplay
6. Chewing gum

7. Sleeping

8. Wrestling

9. Passing notes

10. Walking around

11. Talking to a friend

12. Teasing

Once the list is made, explain to the class that these are not "bad" behaviors but are rather "misplaced" and are not allowed at school. Later, you can refer back to misplaced behaviors as needed.

Examples:

- "Cindy, talking in class is one of those misplaced behaviors. Can you save it for later?"
- "Craig, running out of class is one of those misplaced behaviors. Can you save it for after school? Thanks."

Notes: This strategy allows a teacher to let students know in a nonthreatening way what behaviors are not allowed. It also allows students to know they aren't "bad" for their actions but simply need to postpone the behavior until later.

Strategy: Establish Rules and Consequences

Instructions: Review the list of misbehaviors in chapter 1 and your list of misplaced behaviors. Using the behaviors as a guide, write out up to ten short, easy-to-understand rules similar to these:

Sample Classroom Rules

1. Speak to teachers and fellow classmates with respect.

2. Raise your hand for permission to speak.

3. Remain awake and attentive at all times.

4. Ask permission before leaving your chair.

5. Resolve disagreements by talking.

6. Hand in homework assignments on time.

7. Keep your eyes on your own paper during tests.

8. Respect the property of others.

9. Be on time.

10. Keep all objects to yourself.

Once you have written your rules, make a list of up to five consequences that you have power to enforce, such as:

1. Exclusion from recess

2. Time-out in another class (see chapter 5)

3. Conference with teacher

4. Conference with teacher and principal

5. Call home to parents

6. Time-out in principal's office (see Chapter 5)

7. Conference with teacher, principal, and parents

8. Lunch at time-out table

9. Other: _____

10. Other: _____

Next, rank the consequences from 1 to 5, with the least important being 1 and the most important, 5.

With your rules established and your consequences in order, you are ready to make a tracking chart. The purpose of the chart is to track adherence to the rules. Notice in the sample below that the first three spaces have only the letters A-C in them. These are "free chances." (Please note: Although three free chances may seem like a lot, keep in mind that students often break countless rules and only get yelled at, lectured to, or ignored with no real consequences of any kind.) In other words, if a student breaks a rule, an X is placed in Box A but no privilege is lost (free chances are given because everyone makes mistakes.) Place the five privileges in Boxes D, E, F, G, and H.

If a second rule is broken, an X is placed in Box B, and so on. As the rules are broken and chances used, privileges become jeopardized. In the sample below, an X in Box D would result in the loss of recess.

A	B	C	*Recess* D
Time-out E	*Extra work* F	*Call home* G	*Conference* H

A complete Smart Discipline tracking chart follows at the end of this section. Once rules, consequences, and a sample chart are completed, follow these steps:

Step 1: Fill out the chart and make copies for each student.

Step 2: Pass them out and go over the rules.

Step 3: Explain that if a student breaks a rule, an X will be placed on his or her chart in the box marked A.

Step 4: Explain that if other rules are broken, more Xs will be placed on their charts.

Step 5: Explain that the letters A, B, and C will be "free chances" because everyone makes mistakes.

Step 6: Explain that if Boxes D, E, F, G, and H have Xs, then the consequences listed in those boxes will be enforced.

Step 7: Explain that at the end of the day, students who broke rules will have to bring their charts home for the parents to look at and sign.

Step 8: Explain that when they bring back their charts the next morning, they will receive new ones.

Guidelines:

1. Although consistency is a must, being too picky is a no-no. Be reasonable.

2. When a rule is broken, unemotionally tell the student which rule was broken and put an X on his or her chart.

3. If you don't know which child broke a rule, ask one time. If you are still unsure, give each child involved an X.

4. Refrain from giving warnings or second chances (these are built into the system).

5. When giving a child a new chart the next day, fill out the "Rule of the Day" (which is the rule you want the child to focus on most) and fill out the section "Good Job Yesterday on."

6. Consequences, when possible, should take place that day or, at the latest, the next day.

7. Start over each day.

8. Severe behavior may warrant bypassing the system and going to your "Plan B" strategies.

9. Save your charts so you can get a sense of the progress (or lack thereof) that each student is making.

Notes: Although this strategy takes time to set up, in practice it doesn't take much time to use. One good thing about it is that most children respond very quickly and take control over their behavior.

Another good thing about the system is that it provides for specific information for the parents. Having the charts to refer to if subsequent conferences are necessary is a plus too.

This system can easily be adapted for use in your particular classroom. For example, to save time you might copy the charts with the rules already in place. Or you could allow your students to copy the rules each day in order to reinforce their understanding. You might want to consider other time-saving ideas, such as laminating the charts so they can be used multiple times. Another possibility is to use the charts only with students who need and can benefit most from a structured discipline system.

Use your own creative ideas to make whatever adjustments you need. Practicality is the name of the game.

By the way, this system of discipline is based on my *Smart Discipline*™ system for parents. It is becoming one of the most widely used systems of discipline in America today (so much for being modest!).

Rule violations should be tied to specific consequences.

Smart Discipline Tracking Chart

_____   _____
            Student's Name   Teacher's Name

Classroom Rules:

       1. _____

       2. _____

       3. _____

       4. _____

       5. _____

       6. _____

       7. _____

A	B	C	D
E	F	G	H

Rule of the Day _____

Good Job Yesterday on _____

Note to Parents: Your child has broken some rules today that I thought you should know about. In the chart above, I have circled the rules broken. The Xs indicate how many times rules were broken and the resulting consequences.

Please sign this form below and have your child turn it back in tomorrow or on the next school day. Please let me know if you have questions.

_____   _____
            Parent's Signature   Date

Comments: _____
_____

Strategy: Brainstorm With Peers

Instructions: Brainstorm actions that you have taken in the past with students that helped gain their cooperation. If possible, do this exercise with other teachers and pool your ideas.

Ideas for Prevention

1. _____
2. _____
3. _____
4. _____
5. _____
6. _____
7. _____
8. _____
9. _____
10. _____

Notes: Pick out the ideas that you want to incorporate in your personal *Smart Discipline* Plan. List them under Prevention Strategies on page 110. Remember to include all the ideas you liked from the prevention strategies presented in this section. Include those that worked for you and other teachers in the past.

5

Strategies for Minor Misbehaviors ("Plan A")

Plan A strategies are designed to work on common disruptive behaviors that any student might exhibit. They could range from pencil tapping to whispering to throwing things and so on.

Also, Plan A methods, although quick and easy to use, should produce immediate results. By just using one or two of them, the misbehaving student should stop the offensive behavior right away and redirect his or her attention to the learning task at hand. More important, little if any time needs to be taken away from teaching to employ these techniques.

As you review these strategies, keep in mind that some will work wonders with some students but not at all with others. Don't be distressed by this; just try something else until you find what works with that child. Also, remember that some of these techniques will fit your teaching style and personality better than others. List the ones that you like in your personal Smart Discipline Plan under Plan A Strategies on page 111.

Strategy: Use Friendly Evil Eye

> *Instructions:* Make eye contact with the misbehaving student, smile, and shake head slightly.

> *Notes:* Keep this nonthreatening by smiling. Don't let it interrupt your teaching.

Strategy: Invade Space

Instructions: Keep teaching while you walk over and stand by the offending student. Don't bother to make eye contact, but smile and continue teaching.

Notes: A majority of students will stop misbehaving just so you'll vacate their space.

Strategy: Touch Shoulder

Instructions: While invading space as above, rest your hand on the student's shoulder as you continue to smile and teach.

Notes: The smile and the touch give a powerful nonverbal message that you care about the student and are asking in a friendly way for the wrongful behavior to be ceased.

Beware of the students who react adversely to touch. If a student pulls away and says something like, "Leave me alone; I didn't do anything!" simply whisper, "We'll talk about it later" and move away from the student.

Strategy: Whisper Technique

Instructions: Walk close enough to the student to whisper something like, "Cindy, would you please spit out your gum?" Don't wait for a response. Assume the answer is yes by quickly saying "Thank you," breaking eye contact, and moving away.

Notes: The Whisper Technique conveys to the student the messages that

1. You are not afraid.
2. You care about the student.

    3.   You don't want to embarrass anyone.

    4.   You accept the student, but not the behavior.

    5.   You don't want to get into an argument.

    6.   You trust the student to willingly comply.

By breaking eye contact and moving away quickly, you short-circuit possible power struggles. Maintaining eye contact and staying in the student's space gives the message that you don't trust the student to comply and you are there to force him or her to do so. The opposite message is given when you whisper your request, break eye contact, and move away. This strategy will most likely achieve willing compliance.

Strategy: Smile and Request

Instructions: Either by whispering or by speaking to the student in private, ask the student if he or she would consider changing the behavior. Say, "Thank you" and vacate the student's space.

Examples:

- "Greg, would you consider not drumming your fingers on your desk? Thank you."
- "Mandy, would you consider taking off that head visor? Thank you."

Notes: Most of us will respond positively to someone who smiles at us and asks us to consider doing something. It works like a charm, especially when compared to telling someone to do something.

When seeking a change in behavior from a strong-willed child, the "Smile and Request" strategy is a must. With these kids, and those with oppositional disorders, commands will result in power struggles nearly every time. However, a smiling request most often will result in a positive response.

Strategy: Allow Thinking Time

Instructions: When a student makes a request that you will most likely deny, respond instead with, "Let me think about it. I'll let you know later."

Notes: Employing this strategy has two major advantages.

1. You don't have to stop teaching.
2. You avoid arguments and power struggles.

It also does, in fact, give you some time to consider the request and your response. This is good because if sometimes a quick "no" later turns to a "yes," it teaches a child to keep arguing until the child gets his or her way.

Plus, given time to think, you may come up with an alternative response satisfactory to both parties. One other benefit is that students tend to be "good as gold" while you're considering their requests.

For this to work as an ongoing strategy, occasionally you will have to grant permission. To make sure this happens, you can also respond with "Let me think about it" to some requests you are sure to grant.

Strategy: Change Locations

Instructions: Purposely leave a desk open near the front of the room but still in line with the other desks. When a student misbehaves, whisper to him, "Brad, would you mind sitting over here? Thank you." Move away and go on teaching.

If the student does not comply, go back over and whisper, "Brad, did I ask you in a polite way? Good. Thank you for cooperating."

If still noncompliant, say, "Brad, I see you didn't move. We'll talk about it later." Smile, move away, and go back to teaching.

Notes: Most students will comply right away. When they move, their behavior will change at least for a while. Changing locations causes a child to stop doing what he or she is doing in order to get oriented to the new location.

If a student refuses to comply, withdraw and let yourself and the student out of the power struggle. Make an appointment to discuss the situation later. Trying to force the issue is a real loser for everyone involved as power struggles distress the whole class and can even end up in violence.

Later, when you can speak to the student alone, discuss what happened. Be sure to indicate future consequences for noncompliant behavior.

Strategy: Exercise the Quiet Signal

Instructions: Explain to the class that when you want the whole class to be in their seats and completely quiet, you will raise your hand. Explain that when they see your hand go up, everyone is to return to their seats, raise their hands, and keep them up until everyone is seated and quiet with their hands up.

Notes: Elementary-grade students enthusiastically respond to this method. It saves on your voice, too!

Strategy: State Your Want

Instructions: Once you have the class quiet and paying attention, state what you need for them to do.

Examples:

- "What I want right now is for everyone to work quietly on his or her assignment."

- "What I need right now is for everyone to listen to my instructions."

Notes: Clear and concise statements of needs can often get a class back on track after involvement in highly participatory (and noisy) activities. A very nice pattern of expectancy can be set up by using this strategy with the "Quiet Signal." In other words, if you start using the "Quiet Signal" and always follow it with a statement of what you want, students will quickly get used to your calm and "in charge" approach.

Strategy: Give Information

Instructions: Point out what you are observing at the moment. Simply report the information to the student and do not give instructions.

Examples:

- "Dawn, you were 5 minutes late this morning."
- "John, I didn't get your makeup work."
- "Kerry, you were running in the hall."

Notes: By simply giving information, harsh feelings are avoided. Best of all, the teacher-student relationship is actually strengthened when the teacher shows that he or she is trusting that the student will figure out by himself or herself what needs to be done.

Strategy: Convey Qualities Plus Expectations

Instructions: When a student misbehaves, label the child with a positive quality and tell the child you expect him or her to act that quality out in a certain way.

Examples:

- "Ann, you are an honest person. I expect you to be truthful."
- "Clint, you have good manners. I expect you to be polite."
- "Katie, you are a cooperative person, and I need you to cooperate with me right now."

Notes: Being labeled with a positive attribute startles students. It's something rarely done. Maybe this is why it works so well. Besides gaining compliance, this strategy also builds self-esteem while strengthening the teacher-student relationship. I highly recommend using it liberally.

Do not make the mistake many teachers make. That is, they stop themselves from using this technique. If the student's behavior doesn't always measure up, some teachers feel that focusing on that quality would be a lie. Others feel that telling a student he or she has a certain quality will cause the child to think the child doesn't need to improve.

In response, I would point out that every child possesses both the positive and negative of every quality. The quality they end up believing themselves to possess is mainly determined from feedback from others. Therefore, adults can greatly assist children in adopting positive qualities by assigning the quality to the child as if it were fact.

Label a person with a positive attribute and you give that person something to live up to. For many, you can help create a self-fulfilling prophecy.

Strategy: Give Choices

Instructions: For strong-willed children, this method is especially effective. The children need a sense of control, so you give it to them by giving them choices.

Examples:

- "Brian, would you rather go back to your seat and do your work there, or would you rather do it at the empty desk over here?"
- "Lucinda, would you rather cooperate with me right now and be able to go out for recess, or would you rather sit in the principal's office during recess?"
- "Bonnie, would you rather apologize to Bruce now or make an appointment to talk with me about it during lunch time?"

Notes: If the student either doesn't respond or says "I don't know," simply say, "Sounds like we need to talk about it later; let's make an appointment for 3:05."

For the most effective use of this strategy, remember to smile and be friendly. Your positive energy will produce positive results.

Strategy: Respect the Struggle

Instructions: With this strategy, you show empathy for how difficult it is to control certain behaviors and request future cooperation.

Examples:

- "Jennifer, I understand that it is difficult to control your temper when you get teased. May I count on you to control your temper for the rest of the day?"
- "Frank, I know how hard it is to concentrate when we just have a few hours left before Christmas vacation starts. Would you consider staying in your seat while we finish our math lesson? Thank you."

Notes: When individuals perceive that someone understands their struggles, they feel appreciated. When they feel appreciated, they will likely cooperate. The trick is making sure your empathy is real. Students have an uncanny ability to discern whether or not someone is being sincere. If you are sincere, your students will know it and will respond with cooperation.

Strategy: Answer Questions With Questions

Instructions: Some students have unceasing questions. Some ask absurd questions. Others ask questions they already know the answer to or could find out the answer to with minimal effort.

A teacher can both save time and teach self-reliance by answering questions with questions as in the examples below.

Examples:

Student (for the third time):   "When are we going to start our party?"

Teacher: "What time do you think?"

Student: "How do you spell 'achieve'?"

Teacher: "How could you find out?"

Student: "Do I have to type my report?"

Teacher: "What do you suppose?"

Notes: Consistent use of "Answering Questions With Questions" will give the whole class the message that you expect them to be self-reliant. However, make sure you shoot your questions back in a friendly manner.

Inherent in this strategy is the danger of coming across as a sarcastic or uncaring person. This would be counterproductive. To guard against this, when the student

Respect the struggle by explaining,
"Anything worth doing is worth doing poorly, until we practice enough to do it well."

answers your question appropriately, respond with a smile, a pat on the shoulder, and a kind word.

For those few students who keep coming back with questions (probably for the attention), when you run either out of patience or out of time, ask the student, "Would you consider not asking me any more questions for today?" If you can carry this out while being nice about it, you'll be surprised with the results.

An added touch is to tell the student as he or she is leaving for the day that you appreciated the student cooperating with you. This way, the student goes home feeling good and comes back the next day eager to cooperate with you again.

Strategy: Do Research

> ***Instructions:*** For the next two weeks, ask other teachers the question, "What works best for you to deal with _____?" Fill in the blank with one of the behaviors you listed in chapter 1 on page 8. Take the strategies that appeal to you and list them in your personal *Smart Discipline* Plan.

> ***Notes:*** Over the years, teachers come up with their own "bag of tricks" to gain cooperation in the classroom. Typically, the methods that teachers continually use are the ones that consistently get immediate results and are quick and easy to use. Most teachers are more than willing to share what works for them. All you need to do is ask.

Please note: Review the Plan A strategies that appeal to you and make note of them on your personal Smart Discipline *Plan on page 111.*

6

Strategies for the Most Difficult Misbehaviors ("Plan B")

Plan B strategies are for use with a particular student who continuously acts out despite the use of prevention and Plan A strategies. Typically, these are the students who get labeled as "problem students," "troublemakers," "defiant," "ADHD," "oppositional," or simply "out of control."

These are the students who truly are at risk. If some way cannot be found to motivate them to adopt behaviors and beliefs conducive to learning, they will end up dropping out. In the meantime, they will spend most of their time disrupting the class.

Therefore, for the sake of the student, the teacher, and the rest of the class, an effective plan of discipline must motivate the student to:

1. Follow school rules

2. Cooperate with the teacher

3. Desire to learn

Simply controlling a student's behavior is not enough. Compliance, cooperation, and learning must result for a student to be successful in school.

As with the prevention and Plan A strategies, keep in mind that some Plan B strategies will fit your teaching and personality style better than others. Make a mental note of the ones that appeal to you and also record them in your personal *Smart Discipline* Plan on page 111.

Strategy: Write a Note

Instructions: Write a note to the student describing the problem. Request in the note what action you would like the student to take.

Examples:

Carmen—I have noticed lately that you have been out of your seat without permission. Would you please raise your hand and get permission before getting out of your seat? Thank you.

Ms. Simpson

Terry—This morning you wore your sunglasses in class. Would you consider not wearing them in my class? Thank you.

Mr. Viator

Bev—Your makeup work hasn't been handed in. Would you please have it in by tomorrow? Thanks.

Mr. Crawford

Notes: What do you expect students will do when they get notes like these? Most likely, they will comply. If they don't, there are no hard feelings or power struggles. You simply try something else.

Strategy: Express Strong Feelings

Instructions: In private, completely out of sight and hearing of other students, strongly express your feelings and ask for what you want.

Examples:

- "Brittney, I got very angry when you shoved Cheryl in the hall. May I count on you not to shove other students?"

Our love, trust, and admiration go to those who listen to us.

- "Jeremy, I get extremely frustrated when you keep getting out of your seat. Would you please stay in your seat the rest of the day?"
- "Chris, when you are disrespectful to me I see red. May I count on you to be polite with me?"

Notes: Do not justify your feelings or request. Keep it short and to the point. If the student tries to blame someone else, respond with, "Yes, I understand what you are saying; however, can I count on you to _____?"

If the student wants to draw you into an argument, back out of it, saying, "Sounds like this needs to be discussed further. Let's talk about it at 3:00 this afternoon. Can you come then, or would tomorrow at 12:45 be better?"

Some will take you up on your offer to talk. Those who do could most likely benefit from either a mini-counseling or cooperative planning session. These are the next two strategies.

Strategy: Arrange Mini-Counseling Session

Instructions: Arrange to speak with the misbehaving student where you can sit face-to-face without a desk between you. Start off by saying something like:

- "Stephanie, usually when students aren't cooperating with me, they have a personal reason. Would you like to discuss your reason or would you rather keep it to yourself?"

If she opts to not talk about it, respond with, "It's OK not to talk about it. I just wanted you to know I'm here if you want to talk. In the meantime, may I count on your cooperation?"

If she does want to talk, ask open-ended questions and clarify feelings. Keep it to less than 5 minutes, and invite her to tell you if she would like to talk again.

Notes: Some kids act out in the classroom in reaction to what is going on in their personal lives. Just having someone who cares enough to listen can make a major difference in the student's life and classroom behavior.

If more than a couple of these sessions are needed or if significant problems are mentioned, consult with the school counselor about referring the student for help.

Strategy: Schedule Cooperative Planning Session

Instructions: Make an appointment to meet in private with the student. Describe to the student how you see the problem. Ask for the student's thoughts on how it could be solved.

Examples:

Teacher: "Jason, I'm glad you came in for your appointment. I want to talk about how after lunch you seem to not pay attention to me. It seems like you just stare off into space. What are your thoughts on how you could pay attention to me in the afternoons?"

Student: "I don't know."

Teacher: "Would you like to hear how some other students handle that problem?"

Student: "If I have to."

Teacher: "Well, some students come up and sit in my reserved desk. The change in location seems to help. After a while they go back to their own desk. What do you think?"

Student: "Well, I don't like the idea much. There must be a better way."

Teacher: "OK, let's brainstorm together and write down all the possibilities. Then you can tell me which you like best."

Student: "All right. How about my putting my head down for a
           while or maybe you could come by and let me know if I'm
           spaced out. Sometimes I don't even realize I'm doing it!"

Notes: The difference between the Cooperative Planning Session
and the Mini-Counseling Session strategies is the intent. In the
mini-counseling session, the focus is on getting the student to open
up and talk about what is going on in his or her life. By talking, it
is hoped that either the student will bond with the teacher and
develop a desire to cooperate or will reveal information pertinent
to the student's life that can be dealt with by the school counselor.

The intent of the Cooperative Planning Session is to get the student focused on providing solutions. Occasionally, this approach
works like magic. It's well worth trying.

Strategy: Chart Behavior and Consequences

Instructions: Refer to section titled "Establish Rules and Consequences" on pages 52-58. Be sure to involve the parents by sending
the charts home for their signature.

If the opportunity arises, you may also offer to supply the parents with charts
for them to use at home with their own rules and consequences. Some parents may
jump at the chance. When you think about it, the kids causing you trouble in class are
probably also acting out at home. The parents may be grateful for some suggestions.

Strategy: Use Time-Out

Instructions: Decide on locations for time-out. These may include: (a) a place in the classroom separate from view of the class,
(b) a chair in an upper or lower grade level, or (c) a chair in the
principal's office.

Whisper to the student, "Would you please move to the time-out
area? Thank you." Move away and go back to teaching. If the stu-

dent doesn't go, whisper, "Did I ask you politely? Good, please move to the time-out then." If the child still doesn't go, say privately, "I see you decided not to go. That's OK. We'll talk about it later." Go back to teaching.

Notes: When sending a student to time-out, do not lecture or give work to be done. If using another teacher's room or the principal's office, ask these people not to get into a discussion with the student.

Do not allow the student to take anything to time-out. However, inform the student that he or she can decide to come back when ready to cooperate with the rest of the class.

If the child does not go to time-out after a couple of requests, this may be a signal that you have a very angry or disturbed student on your hands. The worst thing you can do at this point is to try to force the child to do something.

To calm the situation down, you may well want to back off as in the example given above. Or you may want to communicate in a note.

With highly agitated and upset students, be sure to vacate their space and break eye contact. Your main goal is to stay safe by preventing a power struggle and allowing the student time to cool down. Once the student is calm, make an appointment to discuss what happened and future consequences for refusing to move to time-out.

Please note: Any violence or threats of violence should be reported immediately as well as any talk of suicide.

Strategy: Change Volume and Tempo

Instructions: If a student raises his or her voice or is obviously angry and upset, lower your voice and slow your speech down.

Notes: Anger is normally conveyed with a loud voice. The usual way to respond is with a louder voice. This escalates the anger.

If you speak slowly and softly, angry students most likely will follow suit. When they do, they calm down.

A time-out or cool-down period often gives you
and the student time to think about the situation and regain composure.

Strategy: Encourage Student Involvement

Instructions: If a student is highly agitated and will not calm down, ask if the student would be willing to go out in the hall for a while and talk it out with another student. Let the student pick the person, if possible.

Or, if you have a student who is apparently experiencing personal problems, refer the student to a peer counselor, if available. Also consider referrals to school-based support groups or anger management programs.

Other students can also be involved to help with withdrawn students. This can be accomplished by requesting that an outgoing student or group of students help by going out of their way to include the withdrawn student. This can make a powerful difference in a kid's life.

Strategy: Build Relationships

Instructions: With your problem students, be sure to concentrate on building your relationship with them. To do so, review and enact some of the appropriate relationship-building methods described in the chapter on prevention strategies. These included:

1. Welcome Students (see page 38)
2. Express Appreciation (see page 38)
3. Write a Note (see page 40)
4. Write a Letter (see page 40)
5. Call Home (see page 42)
6. Ask Personal Questions (see page 43)
7. Transpose Critical Comments (see page 44)
8. Point Out Talents (see page 45)

9.   Predict Success (see page 47)

10. Elicit Third-Party Encouragement (see page 50)

Notes: Problem students usually draw huge amounts of negativity from authority figures. As they do so, relationships deteriorate as does the student's desire to cooperate with the education process.

What a relief it is for a student with problems when you take the time and effort to build a positive relationship with him or her. Such a relief, in fact, that it can fuel the student with the encouragement necessary to turn his or her attitude and behavior around.

Strategy: Use Activities for Leverage

Instructions: If the misbehaving student participates in sports, band, cheerleading, or any other extracurricular activity, consult with the teacher in charge. Agree on classroom rules that must be followed for the student to participate in the activities on a given day.

In other words, if the student doesn't follow the rules on any certain day, the student does not participate in that day's practice or activity. The student starts over with a new chance the next day. Make sure you inform the parents of your plans and enlist their cooperation.

Notes: For some students, activities are so important that they will do anything to participate, including cooperating with classroom rules.

Follow-through is a must with this strategy. Sticking to disallowing participation can be tough when a big event is scheduled. If the student is allowed to participate regardless of rule violations, the student will learn that he or she can operate in the classroom with impunity.

Therefore, before employing this strategy, decide whether or not you (and the coach) are willing to "stick to your guns." If so, leveraging activities may be just the strategy you need to gain a student's positive cooperation.

Strategy: Analyze and Plan

Instructions: When perplexed about what to do next with a student after you have tried a number of strategies to no avail, it's time to analyze the problem and write out a plan of action. As you do so, answer these questions:

1. What are the behaviors in need of change?
2. What are the expected behaviors?
3. What have I tried?
4. What worked?
5. What didn't work?
6. What are three strategies I could try next?

Notes: You are welcome to photocopy the following worksheet. Sometimes writing things out can help. Be sure to save your worksheets to refer to if conferences are needed.

Smart Discipline
Problem Analysis and Plan of Action

Student's Name: _____   Date: _____

Teacher's Name: _____   Class: _____

1. List the student's most frequent problem behaviors.

    A. _____   D. _____
    B. _____   E. _____
    C. _____   F. _____

2. List the desired behaviors.

    A. _____   D. _____
    B. _____   E. _____
    C. _____   F. _____

3. List strategies that have been tried.

    A. _____
    B. _____
    C. _____
    D. _____

4. List strategies that work with this student.

    A. _____
    B. _____
    C. _____
    D. _____

5. List strategies that have not been successful.

    A. _____
    B. _____
    C. _____

6. List three strategies to try next.

    A. _____
    B. _____
    C. _____

Strategy: Inform Parents

Instructions: Call the student's parents and say to them, "I would like to tell you what behaviors I have been seeing in the classroom so I can get your thoughts." Describe the behaviors and ask, "Can you suggest anything that might help encourage your child to co-operate at school?"

Notes: Do not tell students you will be calling. Parents typically believe whomever they hear from first. And you can be sure if students know you will be calling, they will run home to explain their version of how they have been treated so unfairly. If students don't know you are calling, you won't have to overcome this obstacle.

When speaking with the parents, stay away from labels and blame. Neither is productive.

Strategy: Give Responsibilities

Instructions: Use your creativity to come up with ways the problem student can assist you or others around school. Once decided on, ask the student, "Would you consider helping me with _____?"

Notes: Most students will say yes. When they say yes, they are at the same time agreeing to cooperate with you. Amazingly enough, this can establish a pattern of continued cooperation.

Strategy: Encourage Involvement

Instructions: Encourage problem students to get involved with organized school activities. Volunteer to help get them started or get another student to help facilitate the process.

Sometimes parents don't have the foggiest idea of what's really going on at school. Direct communication with parents is often a must to solve problems.

Notes: Remember that uncooperative students normally have low self-esteem and often believe "I don't have what it takes to be successful in school." Because of their negative beliefs, few participate in extracurricular activities. Also, because of these same beliefs, they need someone behind them to encourage them.

The payoff for getting a student to participate can be big. It has the potential of getting the student to see himself or herself in a more positive light. It may even instill a desire to come to school!

Strategy: Plan for Amends

Instructions: If a student does something for which he or she needs to make amends, make an appointment to discuss the matter. Ask the student how he or she plans to make things right. If the student responds with "I don't know," come back with "Would you like me to tell you how other students make things right when they do the same thing you did?" List the alternatives and ask if the student has any other suggestions.

Once the alternatives are laid out, ask the student to pick one. Agree on when the student will do it and how you will know it was done.

Notes: Too many students continually misbehave and nothing happens. No consequences are faced or amends made. When this happens, it's too bad for the teacher and the student.

It is too bad for the teacher because unchecked disruptive behavior escalates. It is too bad for the student because the student will eventually meet up with inescapable consequences. If his or her behavior has gotten way out of line, those consequences may ruin the student's life.

Lucky is the student who has a teacher who enforces consequences and insists amends be made, where appropriate.

Strategy: Deliver "I" Messages

Instructions: Design a three-part message to deliver to a student about his or her behavior. Plan it in advance and deliver the message in private.

The three parts should include (a) a description of the problem behavior, (b) the feelings that the behavior stirs in you, and (c) the results of the behavior.

Examples:

1. "I noticed you passing notes."
2. "It irritates me when students don't pay attention in class."
3. "When I get irritated, it's tough for me to teach and I lose my patience."

Notes: If the student says, "Who cares?" respond with, "I just wanted you to know." Avoid telling the student what to do about it. Not telling the student what to do prevents backlash and gives the message that the student is intelligent enough to figure out a plan of action.

Strategy: Assign Student Essay

Instructions: Give the problem student the assignment of writing an essay. In the essay, ask the student to answer the following questions:

1. What was the problem in class today?
2. How did you feel during and after the problem took place?
3. What did you do about the problem?
4. How did it work?
5. What will you do next time the problem comes up?

Ask the student to turn in the report the next school day. When handed in, make an appointment to discuss it.

Notes: This strategy has good potential for helping students develop insight into their behavior. It also can provide a constructive method for the students to explain their viewpoint. This can help students calm down and provide a release for their anger.

As an added benefit, a student with a plan of how to handle a problem in the future will more likely do so than a student without a plan. The essay assignment provides a means for this to happen along with a starting point to discuss other possible options for problem resolution.

Strategy: Form a *Smart Discipline* Support Group

Instructions: If your school already has a *Smart Discipline* Support Group for teachers, present your problem student to the group and brainstorm solutions.

Seek out strategies that other teachers have used successfully with this particular student. Find out what other approaches different teachers have used successfully with similar students.

For best results, use the *Smart Discipline* Problem Analysis and Plan of Action form on page 82 of this chapter to present your problem student. Although it can be beneficial to use this forum to vent your frustration, be sure you come away with several concrete suggestions that you would feel comfortable using.

Notes: If your school doesn't have a *Smart Discipline* Support Group, start one. You will be doing yourself, other teachers, and lots of students a big favor.

For additional information on how to start a *Smart Discipline* Support Group call my office at 1-800-538-7107. Ask at the same time about the *Smart Discipline Newsletter.*

Strategy: Consult With Principal and Counselor

Instructions: Set up a meeting between yourself, the principal, and the school counselor. Present your documentation of the student's behavior and your actions to date. Brainstorm and set up a plan of action.

Notes: Make this a formal meeting, not a hasty discussion on the run. Document what was talked about and agreed on.

For the most part, meetings with the principal and counselor will come after trying numerous other strategies without achieving positive results. However, there are some exceptions. You will want to consult with the principal immediately in the following cases:

1. Evidence or suspicion of abuse

2. Evidence or threats of violence

3. Evidence of suicide attempts or threats

Make a verbal report immediately. It is a good idea to follow up with a brief written report of which you keep a copy.

Strategy: Schedule a Meeting With the Principal, Counselor, Parents, Student, and Yourself

Instructions: Accomplish the following three things at this meeting:

1. Agree on setting up an evaluation for the student with the school psychologist.

2. Agree on behaviors that will cause suspension. If possible, arrange for in-house suspension.

3. Ask parents to coordinate consequences at home with behavior at school. Suggest use of the *Smart Discipline* tracking charts. (See page 58. You may make photocopies of these.)

Notes: Both the student and the parents need to get the idea from this meeting that (a) further misconduct of the type discussed will result in suspension and (b) the school desires to provide the help necessary for the student to be successful.

By the time things progress to this event, the prognosis is usually not very good. Sometimes a meeting like this can get a student in touch with the help he or she needs to turn the situation around. With some students, it may make the difference between their ending up in college or in prison.

What a joy it is to take part in helping a student turn away from a path of self-destruction. It is worth every bit of effort that you have to put into the process!

Please note: Review the Plan B strategies that you feel comfortable with and make note of them on your Smart Discipline *Plan on page 111.*

7

Attention Deficit Hyperactivity Disorder (ADHD) Strategies

Before getting into the strategies that work for students with ADHD, review the following points.

1. ADHD is marked by (a) impulsivity, (b) inattention, and (c) hyperactivity (fast-paced activity without a purpose). Children with the condition are normally restless, are easily distracted, show poor judgment, and have poor social skills.

2. Students with ADHD often have low self-esteem as a result of the constant negative feedback that their behavior draws to them.

3. "Bad parenting" does not cause ADHD. This is a common myth. Although the causes remain unknown, it cannot be attributed to mistakes in parenting techniques (lots of parents of ADHD children have other highly successful children with normal behavior).

4. ADHD children can change. It takes longer and is more difficult, but normal behavior is within their grasp. Most will need assistance to attain it as their internal controls are underdeveloped. Until they develop, external controls must be provided.

5. Students with ADHD often are very good at escaping from work and consequences for their behavior. Frequently, they are allowed to skate out from under work assignments or con-

sequences because of their disability. This sets up an unfortunate pattern of irresponsibility. Patterns like this can be reversed, but it takes time, effort, and most of all, loads of patience in implementing a well-thought-out plan of action.

6. Established routines help children with ADHD control their behavior. The more predictable their day, the better off they are. Conversely, unpredictability is upsetting to them.

7. ADHD kids need a structured set of rules and consequences. The rules need to be consistently enforced with immediate consequences. Providing this kind of structure and predictability greatly improves the chances of a child's learning to control his or her behavior.

8. ADHD kids are less sensitive to rewards and consequences; therefore, bigger rewards and consequences need to be used. A slower response time can also be expected. More time, effort, and persistence will be needed to respond to a structured system of discipline.

9. When working with an ADHD child, it is possible to work effectively only with one or possibly two behaviors at a time. Trying to change more than this will only result in frustration and failure.

10. Overt reprimands agitate kids with ADHD. In fact, they cause a child to act out further. They respond far more positively to covert reminders and messages about consequences and time-outs.

11. As with any child, behavior is more successfully controlled if the child can expect consequences to be enforced at home as well as at school. An ideal format for accomplishing this is the *Smart Discipline* charting system as described in the chapter on prevention strategies. Communication between school and home will have to occur daily. However, the effort will pay off in much more controlled and productive behavior.

12. Until an ADHD child's behavior is under control, you can expect very little schoolwork or learning to take place. Therefore, priority one is a plan of action to help the child learn how to control his or her behavior. In the meantime, don't set high goals for the output and quality of schoolwork. Doing so will only frustrate you and the child.

13. Do not label a child as having ADHD. Misdiagnosis can cause a child not to receive proper treatment for other possible conditions. Also, the diagnosis of ADHD can be highly upsetting to parents and needs to be dealt with in a professional setting by a physician or mental health professional.

14. Biological intervention with methylphenidate (trade name Ritalin) helps some children with ADHD become less impulsive, less hyper, and more attentive. However, it is not a cure-all. Ritalin cannot be expected to motivate a child to do his or her schoolwork and to follow the rules. This will still have to be done through working closely with the child, addressing one behavior at a time.

15. ADHD kids take great pride in learning how to control their behavior and in achieving goals. And it is a great joy to help them do so.

16. The major goals of working with ADHD students are to get them to think before they act and to control their own behavior. Achieving this takes longer than it does with other kids. However, you can get 80% of the way there with the strategies described in other chapters of this book. The other 20%, given time, patience, and persistence, can be achieved with the following strategies.

Strategy: Choose Close Proximity

Instructions: Choose a seat as close to you as possible for the ADHD student.

Notes: Having the child close to you means you will spend less time responding to his or her behavior. Also, it allows you to easily teach from "the child's space," which helps with behavior control. As with any student, behavior of students sitting close to the teacher is normally better than those sitting further away (at least for kids prone to misbehaving).

Strategy: Set a Desired Behavior

Instructions: Pick out the single behavior that is bothering you the most. Decide what behavior you want instead. Choose three strategies from this and previous chapters that you could use to prompt the desired behavior. Write them down.

Example:

1. Unwanted behavior: Wandering out of seat
2. Desired behavior: To stay in seat unless the child raises hand for permission to be out of seat
3. Strategies to try:
    A. Write a Note.
    B. Enlist Four-Step Time Out (see page 96).
    C. Show Appreciation.

Notes: Remember not to expect immediate results. In fact, you can expect sporadic compliance that will improve over time. Resist the urge to give up and try something else. Stick with your plan for 4 weeks. At that time, assess what worked and what did not. Then, keep what did work and change the rest.

Strategy: Use *Smart Discipline* Chart

Instructions: Same as described under prevention strategies in Chapter 4. Modify the system to include only one or two rules. When those are consistently being followed, add another one.

Notes: If possible, encourage the parent to provide a consequence at home if all of the squares are lost at school. These consequences might include such things as:

1. Loss of TV time
2. Loss of outside play time
3. Loss of bike privileges
4. Earlier bedtime
5. Loss of electronic game playing time
6. Extra chores

If interested in further information, the parent may want to order the *Smart Discipline* Workbook (which describes all of the steps of this system for the home) by calling 1-800-538-7107.

With ADHD students especially, be sure to fill in the blank provided for "Good Job Yesterday on." Ample amounts of encouragement are just as beneficial as providing a solid structure of rules and consequences.

Strategy: Give Covert Reminders

Instructions: When you observe an ADHD student starting into an unacceptable behavior, instead of a harsh reprimand, give a friendly reminder to help the student think before he or she acts.

Example:

- "Jimmy, do you think that's wise?"
- "Brenda, remember what we talked about?"

Rules should be short, simple, and specific.

- "Kyle, what is the rule?"
- "Jan, what is the consequence for that?"

Notes: Be sure to smile and respond by saying "Good thinking" when the student responds positively to your reminder. The purpose, of course, is to help a child to think before he or she acts and for the child to control the his or her own behavior. Because they are different from other kids, many, many more reminders will have to be given to achieve results.

Remember here also that harsh reprimands only aggravate the situation. Although it's tough sometimes not to react angrily to a child's repetitive misbehaviors, the consequence of expressing that anger is to cause further misbehavior. What works are friendly, covert reminders.

Strategy: Encourage After-School Activities

Instructions: Encourage the student to participate in after-school activities such as Scouts, sports, music, art, and drama programs.

Notes: Many children like these activities enough that they will strive very hard to learn to control their behavior in order to participate. Also of benefit are the social skills learned and the insight reached through feedback given by peers.

Strategy: Enlist Four-Step Time-Out

Instructions:

Step 1: Set up four different places to send students for time-out, such as:

A. In the classroom but separate from the rest of the class

B. In the hallway or another teacher's class

C. In a special chair in the principal's office

D. In the student's home

Step 2: Explain to the student what behavior will cause him or her to be sent to time-out. Use only one or two behaviors at a time (pick the most disruptive behaviors first).

Step 3: Explain to the student that the first offense will result in an in-class time-out, the second offense in a hallway time-out, and so on.

Step 4: Ask the parents if they would be willing to pick up their child and put him or her in time-out at home. If this is not possible, brainstorm with the principal on possible alternatives.

Notes: One objection to taking children out of the classroom is that they won't be learning anything. In response to this objection, it should be noted that children aren't learning anything while disrupting the class either. At least by taking them out of the classroom, they are learning that if they break the rule, they will not be allowed to participate with the rest of the class.

Follow through with as much consistency as possible. Do not give a warning once an offense has occurred (unless the child is on a *Smart Discipline* chart with one of the consequences being a time-out. In this case, he or she has three free chances or warnings built into the system). However, if you observe the student starting into a misbehavior, you may want to use a covert reminder to help the child stop himself or herself from breaking the rules.

If the child refuses to move to time-out, say, "I see you decided to stay here. We'll talk about it later." Later, talk about it and impose a consequence like the loss of the next recess. Explain that the same thing will happen if he or she refuses time-out in the future.

Strategy: Respond With One-Liners

Instructions: Respond to repetitive questions and statements with "one-liners." Use them repetitively.

Examples:

Student: "When are we going to have our party?"
Teacher: "When did I tell you?"

Student: "That's not fair!"
Teacher: "Probably so."

Student: "Can I _____?"
Teacher: "Let me think about it."

Student: "Is it lunchtime yet?"
Teacher: "You tell me."

Notes: Say it in a friendly, caring way so you don't come off as being sarcastic. The purpose of this strategy is not to fall into the trap of reinforcing children's repetitive questions by giving them your attention. If you stick with the same one-liners each time, eventually children will stop asking repetitive questions. Be prepared, though, for it to take a while.

Strategy: Refocus

Instructions: Make a list of at least five desirable behaviors and traits that the child has. In a private way, let the child know you noticed his or her positive behavior or trait.

Sample List

1. Punctual
2. Creative
3. Friendly
4. Truthful
5. Intelligent

Sample Statements

1. "John, I noticed you were on time again today. Good job."
2. "Sally, let me tell you what I like about your poster." (Describe what you like.)
3. "Bobby, I noticed you made friends with the new student. That was nice of you."
4. "Craig, I like the way you tell the truth."
5. "Bonnie, you remembered all of the state capitals. You have a good memory."

Notes: Sadly, people who work with ADHD children often get so focused on the "bad behavior" that these children get negative feedback literally heaped on them. As this happens, their self-concept worsens as does their behavior. Lucky is the student who has a teacher willing to take the time and effort to notice and focus on the positive. Their self-concept improves, as does their behavior.

To make your encouragement meaningful, make sure to attach it to evidence. Also, in order not to reinforce some children's addiction to attention, give your positive feedback in private. And, if the child is "fishing for praise," respond with statements such as, "Tell me what you like about your project (or performance)."

If the child responds negatively or with a "poor-me" attitude, resist the urge to talk the child out of it or to point out the positive. Instead, allow the child to have his or her feeling or thought by simply restating the thought or clarifying the feeling, for example, "Sounds like you are dissatisfied with your poster, is that right?" or "It seems like you are angry with yourself, is that right?"

Strategy: Consult With Former Teachers

Instructions: Seek out former teachers and ask what they found worked with a particular student and what did not.

Notes: Beware of the response, "Nothing works with him." If questioned further, most teachers will remember a few things that seemed to work better than others. If not, it does not mean that nothing works. Rather, it means that what works has not yet been found or tried with this particular child.

Consult also with other teachers the student may currently have. Some children with ADHD respond incredibly well to certain teachers. You will want to explore what this teacher is doing differently.

Strategy: Analyze Achievement

Instructions: When a child sometimes behaves appropriately and sometimes does not, see if you can figure out the difference in the conditions that might possibly be influencing the child's choices of behavior. Consider the following in relation to times he or she was behaving as opposed to misbehaving:

1. Were you saying or doing anything different?
2. What was the noise and activity level in the class?
3. What were the times of day?
4. What were the days of week?
5. What activities preceded the behavior?
6. What activities were coming up that day?

Notes: Repeat this exercise and document your answers over a 4-week period. See if any patterns seem to emerge. If possible, question parents about periods of marked good or bad behavior. Get their thoughts as to what might be possible causes.

You will want, of course, to modify conditions that seem to adversely affect behavior and repeat the variables that foster good behavior.

The common objection to this process is time. Teachers say, "I don't have the time for this. I have 30 other kids to teach." They are right, and only the ones who lose enough time from teaching due to disruptive ADHD behavior will be motivated to take the necessary time and effort to implement this strategy.

Strategy: Physical Contact

Instructions: Try making physical contact with

1. Handshakes
2. Pats on the arm or back
3. Resting hand on student's shoulder while teaching

Notes: With some children, touching can create a powerful bond between teacher and student. With the creation of this bond comes a huge desire on the student's part to cooperate with the teacher.

Other students with ADHD may react negatively to touching. If so, don't force it, simply move on to another strategy.

Strategy: Slow Tempo

Instructions: When responding to a child displaying hyperactive behavior, speak very calmly, slowly, and softly.

Notes: Your slower and calmer speech pattern will tend to help the child slow and calm down. This is often tough to do as the natural response to hyperactivity is to loudly and quickly react to the child. This only reinforces the hyperactivity.

Slowing your tempo gives a child more time to think about what he or she is saying and doing. And, if nothing else, it will allow you to stay calm!

Strategy: Assign Predictable Responsibilities

Instructions: Brainstorm chores that need to be done daily in your classroom or school. Ask the child if he or she would help you out by taking on the responsibility of completing that task at a certain time each day.

Notes: Make sure to show the student exactly what needs to be done so the child virtually cannot fail. Do not assign meaningless tasks but rather assign ones where the student can feel he or she is making an important contribution.

Although it is often easier to "do it yourself," you do the ADHD child a big favor by assigning predictable responsibilities. First, it helps a child foster a belief that he or she "has what it takes to be successful." Second, children with ADHD do better when their day is structured and predictable.

Let the parents know what you are doing and why. The possible perception that you are "making the child work" must be avoided.

Strategy: Facilitate Insights

Instructions: When you notice the student displaying the desired behavior, set aside time to ask the student how he or she was able to control their behavior. Also, ask what he or she did differently.

Examples:

- "Phillip, I noticed you stayed in your seat today. How did you do that?"
- "Casey, I noticed that you didn't get into any fights on the playground. What did you do differently today?"

Suggest a structured time for homework.

Notes: If the child responds with "I don't know," give the child some choices such as:

- "Well, was it because you were stuck to your chair or because you decided to stay in it?"
- "Do you think you didn't fight today because you forgot how or because you decided to do other things instead?"

Be sure to make one choice absurd and one that helps point out that the child is in control of his or her behavior. This conversation should be private but can be accomplished without taking much time by limiting the conversation to just a few seconds.

Strategy: Organize a Conference

Instructions: Enlist the school counselor's help in setting up a conference to include all teachers presently working with the child, the parents, the school psychologist, and the principal, if appropriate.

Notes: The purpose of this conference should be to set up an action plan that includes recommendations for appropriate evaluations and referrals to community and school resources. Stay away from blame and labels. Direct all efforts to the delineation of an action plan complete with timeline, assignment or tasks, and method of follow-up.

Please note: Pick out the ADHD strategies that you can make use of and note them in your personal Smart Discipline *Plan under ADHD Strategies. Be sure to include other strategies you have found to be effective with ADHD students.*

8

Your Personal *Smart Discipline* Plan

The major purpose of this book is to provide numerous positive discipline strategies from which a teacher can pick and choose to design a personal *Smart Discipline* Plan. To pull a comprehensive personal plan together, choose from all four categories: (a) prevention strategies, (b) Plan A strategies, (c) Plan B strategies, and (d) ADHD strategies.

A quick reference guide is on the next four pages. Check off the strategies that align with your teaching style and note them on your personal *Smart Discipline* plan on pages 110 and 111. Make sure also to note other strategies that have worked for you and other teachers in the past.

As you fill out your plan, first complete the section provided for the misbehaviors you most frequently encounter along with the behaviors you have the most difficulty correcting. As you pick out the different strategies to include in your plan, make sure they address these behaviors.

For best results, try out one strategy at a time. Once it is consistently working for you, try out another one. By doing this, your *Smart Discipline* strategies will become second nature to you. And best of all, you will become a master of classroom discipline. I guarantee it!

Smart Discipline
Quick Reference Guide

Prevention Strategies

(Check off those that appeal to you and list on page 110.)

- ☐ Welcome Students, page 38
- ☐ Express Appreciation, page 38
- ☐ Write a Note, page 40
- ☐ Write a Letter, page 40
- ☐ Call Home, page 42
- ☐ Ask Personal Questions, page 43
- ☐ Transpose Critical Comments, page 44
- ☐ Point Out Talents, page 45
- ☐ Predict Success, page 47
- ☐ Make Appointments, page 47
- ☐ Elicit Third-Party Encouragement, page 50
- ☐ List Misplaced Behaviors, page 51
- ☐ Establish Rules and Consequences, page 52
- ☐ Use S*mart Discipline* Tracking Chart, page 58
- ☐ Brainstorm With Peers, page 59

Plan A Strategies

(Check off those that appeal to you and list on page 111.)

- ☐ Use Friendly Evil Eye, page 60
- ☐ Invade Space, page 61
- ☐ Touch Shoulder, page 61
- ☐ Whisper Technique, page 61
- ☐ Smile and Request, page 62
- ☐ Allow Thinking Time, page 63
- ☐ Change Locations, page 63
- ☐ Exercise the Quiet Signal, page 64
- ☐ State Your Want, page 64
- ☐ Give Information, page 65
- ☐ Convey Qualities Plus Expectations, page 65
- ☐ Give Choices, page 66
- ☐ Respect the Struggle, page 67
- ☐ Answer Questions With Questions, page 68
- ☐ Do Research, page 70

Plan B Strategies

(Check off those that appeal to you and list on page 111.)

- ☐ Write a Note, page 72
- ☐ Express Strong Feelings, page 72
- ☐ Arrange Mini-Counseling Session, page 74
- ☐ Schedule Cooperative Planning Session, page 75
- ☐ Chart Behavior and Consequences, page 76
- ☐ Use Time-Out, page 76
- ☐ Change Volume and Tempo, page 77
- ☐ Encourage Student Involvement, page 79
- ☐ Build Relationships, page 79
- ☐ Use Activities for Leverage, page 80
- ☐ Analyze and Plan, page 81
- ☐ Inform Parents, page 83
- ☐ Give Responsibilities, page 83
- ☐ Encourage Involvement, page 83
- ☐ Plan for Amends, page 85
- ☐ Deliver "I" Messages, page 86
- ☐ Assign Student Essay, page 86
- ☐ Form a *Smart Discipline* Support Group, page 87
- ☐ Consult With Principal and Counselor, page 88
- ☐ Schedule a Meeting With the Principal, Counselor, Parents, Student, and Yourself, page 88

ADHD Strategies
(Check off those that appeal to you and list on page 111.)

☐ Choose Close Proximity, page 92
☐ Set a Desired Behavior, page 93
☐ Use *Smart Discipline* Chart, page 94
☐ Give Covert Reminders, page 94
☐ Encourage After-School Activities, page 96
☐ Enlist Four-Step Time-Out, page 96
☐ Respond With One-Liners, page 98
☐ Refocus, page 98
☐ Consult With Former Teachers, page 100
☐ Analyze Achievement, page 100
☐ Physical Contact, page 101
☐ Slow Tempo, page 101
☐ Assign Predictable Responsibilities, page 102
☐ Facilitate Insights, page 102
☐ Organize a Conference, page 104

Smart Discipline Plan

_____   _____
Teacher's Name   Date

List the five most frequent misbehaviors you encounter in your class. After you fill out the rest of your plan, come back and fill in "Strategies to Use."

Behaviors   Strategies to Use

1. _____   _____
2. _____   _____
3. _____   _____
4. _____   _____
5. _____   _____

List the three behaviors that are the most difficult for you to correct. As above, fill in the "Strategies to Use" after filling out the rest of your plan.

Behaviors   Strategies to Use

1. _____   _____
2. _____   _____
3. _____   _____

List below the prevention strategies that appeal to you most. Add any reminders or notes.

Prevention Strategies   Notes and Reminders

1. _____   _____
2. _____   _____
3. _____   _____
4. _____   _____
5. _____   _____
6. _____   _____
7. _____   _____
8. _____   _____
9. _____   _____
10. _____   _____

List your Plan A strategies here with notes and reminders. Be sure to add other strategies that have worked either for you or other teachers in the past.

Plan A Strategies	Notes and Reminders
1. _____	_____
2. _____	_____
3. _____	_____
4. _____	_____
5. _____	_____

List below the Plan B strategies you can use. Add to the list suggestions from other teachers as well as ideas from your own experience.

Plan B Strategies	Notes and Reminders
1. _____	_____
2. _____	_____
3. _____	_____
4. _____	_____
5. _____	_____

List here the ADHD strategies that make sense to you. Include anything and everything that might work.

ADHD Strategies	Notes and Reminders
1. _____	_____
2. _____	_____
3. _____	_____
4. _____	_____
5. _____	_____

Please note: Remember to go back to your list of the most frequent and difficult behaviors you encounter and fill in the blanks for "Strategies to Use."

Suggested Readings

Anderson, J. (1981). *Thinking, changing, rearranging*. Portland, OR: Metamorphous.

Axelrod, S. (1977). *Behavior modification for the classroom teacher*. New York: McGraw-Hill.

Bartel, N., & Hammill, D. (1990). *Teaching students with learning and behavior problems* (5th ed.). Boston: Allyn & Bacon.

Baruth, L., & Eckstein, D. (1982). *The ABCs of classroom discipline*. Dubuque, IA: Randall/Hunt.

Brophy, J. (1985). Classroom management as instruction: Socializing and self-guidance in students. *Theory Into Practice, 24,* 233-240.

Canter, L. (1984). *Lee Canter's parent conference book*. Santa Monica, CA: Lee Canter & Associates.

Charles, C. M. (1986). *Building classroom discipline from models to practice* (3rd ed.). White Plains, NY: Longman.

Doyle, W. (1986). Classroom organization and management. In M. C. Wittrock (Ed.), *Handbook of research on teaching*. New York: Macmillan.

Dreikurs, R. (1982). *Maintaining sanity in the classroom*. New York: Harper & Row.

Evertson, C. (1986). Training teachers in classroom management: An experimental study in secondary school classrooms. *Journal of Educational Research, 79,* 51-58.

Fifer, F. (1986). Effective classroom management. *Academic Therapy, 21,* 401-410.

Ginott, H. (1972). *Teacher and child: A book for parents and teachers*. New York: Avon.

Glasser, W. (1978). 10 steps to good discipline. *Today's Education, 66,* 60-63.

Glasser, W. (1986). *Control theory in the classroom*. New York: Harper & Row.

Glasser, W. (1990). *The quality school: Managing students without coercion*. New York: HarperPerennial.

). *Teacher effectiveness training.* New York: Wyden.

l, F. W. (1994). *Creating safe schools: What principals can do.* Thou-
s, CA: Corwin.

The gentle art of classroom discipline. *National Elementary Princi-*
-30.

Positive classroom discipline. New York: McGraw-Hill.

s, F. (1986). *Comprehensive classroom management* (2nd ed.). Boston:
acon.

berg, Z., & Fleisch, B. (1990). *At the schoolhouse door: An examination*
s and policies for children with behavior and emotional problems.
Bank Street College of Education.

). *Discipline and group management in classrooms.* New York: Holt,
& Winston.

se, W. C., & Newman, R. G. (1980). *Conflict in the classroom: The*
of children with problems (4th ed.). Belmont, CA: Wadsworth.

Martin, R. (1980). *Teaching through encouragement.* Englewood Cliffs, NJ: Prentice-
Hall.

McIntyre, T. (1989). *The behavior management handbook: Setting up effective behavior*
management systems. Boston: Allyn & Bacon.

McIntyre, T. (1989). *A resource book for remediating common behavior and learning*
problems. Boston: Allyn & Bacon.

McKay, M., & Fanning, P. (1986). *Self-esteem.* Oakland, CA: New Harbinger.

O'Leary, D., & O'Leary, S. (1977). *Classroom management: The successful use of behav-*
ior modification (2nd ed.). New York: Pergamon.

Podesta, C. (1990). *Self-esteem and the six-second secret.* Newbury Park, CA: Corwin.

Polsgrove, L. (1920). *Reducing undesirable behaviors.* Reston, VA: Council for Exceptional Children.

Quarles, C. L. (1993). *Staying safe at school.* Newbury Park, CA: Corwin.

Rardin, R. (1978, September). Classroom management made easy. *Virginia Journal of*
Education, pp. 14-17.

Rimm, S. B. (1986). *Underachievement syndrome: Causes and cures.* Watertown, WI:
Apple.

Rizzo, J. V., & Zabel, R. H. (1988). *Educating children and adolescents with behavioral*
disorders: An integrative approach. Boston: Allyn & Bacon.

Shevialkov, G., & Redd, F. (1956). *Discipline for today's children.* Washington, DC: Association for Supervision and Curriculum Development.

Short, P., Short, J., & Blanton, C. (1994). *Rethinking student discipline.* Thousand Oaks, CA: Corwin.

Simpson, R. L., et al. (1991). *Programming for aggressive and violent students.* Reston, VA: ERIC.

Will, M. (1986). Educating children with learning problems: A shared responsibility. *Exceptional Children, 52,* 411-416.

Zionts, P. (1985). *Teaching disturbed and disturbing students: An integrative approach.* Austin, TX: Pro-Ed.

CORWIN
PRESS

The Corwin Press logo—a raven striding across an open book—represents the happy union of courage and learning. We are a professional-level publisher of books and journals for K–12 educators, and we are committed to creating and providing resources that embody these qualities. Corwin's motto is "Success for All Learners."

Videotapes, audiotapes, and books available from
Up With Youth
Get your free preview tape now!

Do you have a need to teach parents about discipline or provide parents with self-help resources on discipline?

If so, we invite you to preview our **Up With Parents** videotape and our **Smart Discipline Workbook**™ **for Parents.** The videotape is a two-hour presention of the nationally acclaimed **Up With Parents** Workshop which teaches our **Smart Discipline**™ System. It can be used to help you facilitate *your own* Up With Parents Workshop, or it can be loaned out to parents to view on their own.

Some advantages to **Smart Discipline**™:

- Can be taught in one session
- Easy to use consistently
- Completely affordable, no minimum order
- Highly effective and practical

- Extraordinarily easy for parents to use
- Can be taught in groups, or parents can view the video and work individually with the workbook
- Includes a facilitator's manual free with every order
- No training required

Up With Parents attracts groups of parents ranging in size from 25 to 300. All orders include flyer slicks and a step-by-step guide to promoting the workshop. Call our toll-free number today for your free videotape.

1-800-538-7107

V3010 *Up With Parents Program* - Dr. Koenig presents his nationally acclaimed program for parents of children of any age. This entertaining and innovative program focuses on discipline and self-esteem. Parents learn guaranteed ways to stop fighting and bickering, gain cooperation and instill self-confidence in children.

2-Hour VHS Videotape:
V3010   **$24.95**

2 Audiotapes:
#C2025   **$18.00**

PART TWO:
HOMEWORK: CRITICAL PARENTING GUIDELINES

B1015 Parents' Homework Manual- Ironclad ways to stop nightly struggles over homework forever • How to get your children to do their homework independently • The fifteen biggest homework problems parents encounter and step-by-step solutions • The five most common mistakes parents make over homework • The three homework rules your child needs you to insist upon • How to team up with the teacher for your child's best benefit • How to motivate your children to do their best work • Six sure-fire ways to change negative beliefs and attitudes into positive and productive ones

Parents' Homework Manual: **$15.00**

Our Best-Seller For Parents

B1010 *Smart Discipline* Work-book - Easy to follow and immediately usable. This workbook for parents takes you right through the *Smart Discipline* System, the most effective system of discipline available today. Parents can copy the charts right from the book.

Smart Discipline for Parents: **$12.00**

A1001 *Up With Youth* **Soundtrack by M'Prove** - The nationally acclaimed *Up With Youth* Self-Esteem Music for Kids. This audiotape has all the songs from the *Up With Youth* Seminar and teaches children how to build their own high self-esteem. Children and parents alike love them. For ages 7 and up.

Up With Youth Audiotape: **$12.00**

P.S. We are also seeking people who would like to teach *Up With Parents* to community and church groups. The income potential is $100 to $500 per seminar. Call or write if you would like more information about this option.

More practical programs from Larry Koenig

UP WITH STEPFAMILIES

Dr. Larry Koenig, the author and creator of Up With Youth, the nation's leading self-esteem program for kids, presents his workshop for stepparents on two tape cassettes.

HERE'S WHAT YOU WILL LEARN

- HOW TO BUILD LOVE AND TRUST
- HOW TO TURN HOSTILITY TO COOPERATION
- HOW TO GET FAMILY MEMBERS TO ACCEPT ONE ANOTHER
- WHY JEALOUSY, ANGER, AND RESENTMENT ARE COMMON TO STEP-FAMILIES
- HOW TO DEAL WITH EX-SPOUSES

- WHY KIDS REALLY ACT OUT AFTER A VISIT TO DAD'S
- HOW TO SUCCESSFULLY SURVIVE THE STAGES STEPFAMILIES GO THROUGH
- WHY STEPPARENTS AND STEPCHILDREN HAVE TROUBLE GETTING ALONG AND HOW TO TURN THE TIDE

C2027 Up With Stepfamilies - Finally, here is a straightforward guide to meeting the everyday challenges in stepfamilies. Dr. Koenig gives wonderful insights and concrete solutions to your problems. Full of illuminating examples, expertise and empathy, these tapes will help you and your family immeasurably.

Set of Two Audiotapes: **$18.00**

B1012 The Making of a Happy Family - This book is a wonderful and powerful guide for helping parents build their children's self-esteem. The step-by-step activities in this book will also help you build a strong, loving, cooperative and peaceful family.

The Making of a Happy Family : **$12.00**

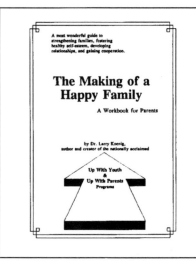

The Making of a Happy Family
A Workbook for Parents

by Dr. Larry Koenig, author and creator of the nationally acclaimed

Up With Youth & Up With Parents Programs

Self-Hypnosis for Success and Happiness & The Ultimate Relaxation and Stress Reduction Tape

by Larry Koenig 1991

C2020 Self-Hypnosis, Relaxation, and Stress Reduction -Includes two audiotapes: one for self-hypnosis to enrich your own self-esteem and happiness, the other to induce a wonderful state of relaxation and whisk away the stress in your life. An excellent aid for sleeping, too.

Set of Two Audiotapes: **$18.00**

F6633 Arith-Magic Flash Cards - Puts math facts into all 3 forms of memory: Auditory, Visual, and Kinesthetic. Teaches facts in "Number Families" at the same time. Kids love them!

Flash Cards for Addition & Subtraction:
#F6633-1 **$7.50**

Flash Cards for Multiplication & Division:
#F6633 -2 **$7.50**

#F6633 Both Sets: **$14.00**

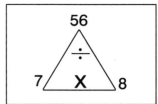

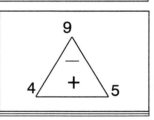

To order or get **FREE** information, complete the coupon and
Fax: 1-504-291-3532 OR Call: 1-800-538-7107

MAIL TO: *UP WITH YOUTH*
11758 S. Harrell's Ferry Road, Ste C
Baton Rouge, LA 70816

UP WITH YOUTH ORDER FORM

To charge to your Mastercard® or Visa® or to order with a purchase number, please fill out this form and indicate the the merchandise being ordered.

- ❏ Please bill to (circle one) MasterCard® / Visa®

  Card Number _____

  Expiration Date _____

- ❏ Purchase Order Number #_____
- ❏ Check Enclosed

(Please Print)

Name: _____ Title _____

Name of Business or School: _____

Street Address: _____

City _____ State _____ Zip _____

Daytime: ( ) _____

Qty.	Item Code	Item	Price	Total
☐	V3010	Up With Parents VHS Videotape	$24.95	_____
☐	C2025	Up With Parents Audiotapes	$18.00	_____
☐	B1015	Homework Manual- Critical Parenting Guidelines	$15.00	_____
☐	B1010	Smart Discipline Workbook (for Parents)	$12.00	_____
☐	A1001	Up With Youth Soundtrack	$12.00	_____
☐	C2027	Up With Stepfamilies Audiotapes	$18.00	_____
☐	B1012	The Making of a Happy Family Workbook	$12.00	_____
☐	C2020	Self-Hypnosis, Relaxation & Stress Reduction	$18.00	_____
☐	F6633-1	Arith-Magic Flash Cards Addition & Subtraction	$ 7.50	_____
☐	F6633-2	Arith-Magic Flash Cards Multiplication & Division	$ 7.50	_____
☐	F6633	Arith-Magic Flash Cards (Both Sets)	$14.00	_____

Add 10% shipping and handling (minimum $4.00) _____

LA residents add 8% sales tax. _____

TOTAL . . . . . . _____

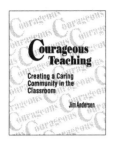

Here's more expert help from Corwin Press

Mastery Teaching
Increasing Instructional Effectiveness in Elementary, Secondary Schools, Colleges, and Universities

Madeline Hunter

Madeline Hunter was one of the most well-respected and widely known advocates of professional development for educators. Her passion and dedication are evident in every line of text, and her skillful presentation of her concepts will inspire you — regardless of whether you're a veteran administrator or are new to the teaching profession.

Mastery Teaching, her most popular book, has sold 100,000 copies worldwide and is still going strong. Learn the essentials of effective instruction for students at every ability level. Techniques and examples are described in full detail, including inservice plans for groups and individuals.

© 1982, 124 pages
D5856-6264-9 (Paperback)   **$17.95**

A Handbook for Teacher Leaders

Leonard O. Pellicer
Lorin W. Anderson
University of South Carolina

"*A Handbook for Teacher Leaders* is a readable, engaging book that is refreshingly free from jargon. A must read for teachers and all who are concerned with improving the educational process and who want to understand more about teaching and learning and how to use this knowledge to change schools."

Ann Lieberman, Professor
Teachers College, Columbia University

Whether you are a leader on the practitioner level, a staff developer, or are involved in teacher preparation courses, this book provides invaluable tools to help you foster high performance in yourself and others.

© 1995, 264 pages
D5856-6172-3 (Hardcover)   **$45.95**
D5856-6173-1 (Paperback)   **$22.95**

ORDER FORM   D5856

CORWIN PRESS, INC.
A Sage Publications Company
2455 Teller Road
Thousand Oaks, CA 91320-2218
e-mail: order@corwin.sagepub.com
Call: 805-499-9774 Fax: 805-499-0871

FAX YOUR ORDER!
805-499-0871
or call:
805-499-9774

SageFax 100

Ship to

Name_____

Institution _____

Address_____

City _____ State _____ ZIP _____

Telephone (We call *only* in case of problems) (_____)_____

Bill to (if different)   (Please attach P.O. to this form.)

Institution _____

Attn. _____

Address_____

City _____ State _____ ZIP _____

Method of Payment

☐ Check, #_____   ☐ VISA® ☐ MasterCard® ☐ Bill me*

Account No. _____   Exp. Date _____

_____
Signature

Smart Discipline for the Classroom
☐ Paperback, **D5856-6341-6** **$19.95**
Courageous Teaching
☐ Paperback, **D5856-6239-8** **$19.95**
The Least of These
☐ Hardcover, **D5856-6200-2** **$39.95**
☐ Paperback, **D5856-6201-0** **$19.95**
Self-Esteem and the Six-Second Secret
☐ Paperback, **D5856-6037-9** **$15.00**
Becoming a Teacher Leader
☐ Paperback, **D5856-6087-5** **$11.95**
Mastery Teaching
☐ Paperback, **D5856-6264-9** **$17.95**
A Handbook for Teacher Leaders
☐ Hardcover, **D5856-6172-3** **$45.95**
☐ Paperback, **D5856-6173-1** **$22.95**

☐ Please send me your complete (free) catalog.

Total of books ordered: _____
In CA, add 7.25% Sales Tax*   _____
In IL, add 6.25% Sales Tax*   _____
In MA, add 5% Sales Tax*   _____
In Canada, add 7% GST*   _____
Subtotal   _____
Handling*   _____$2.00____
Amount Due   _____

* Note: Payment or credit card information must accompany orders under $25.00.
Handling (a $2.00 flat processing fee added to all orders) *plus* actual shipping costs are added to billed orders. Prices subject to change without notice. **In Canada, please add 7% Goods & Services Tax #R129786448 and remit in U.S. Funds.** Thank you.

 Corwin Press, Inc., 2455 Teller Road, Thousand Oaks, CA 91320-2218